inperspective

danholm/photosandperspectives

IN PERSPECTIVE

ISBN 978-1-4303-0517-0

Published by Lulu.com

For mom and dad.

introduction

Whenthe first pictures of earth were beamed back from space, we saw something nobody in the history of mankind had ever seen before. For the very first time, we caught a glimpse of ourselves from an entirely new perspective. To actually step back and see our planet hanging in the middle of nowhere shed new light on who we are, how we see ourselves and how we fit into the grand scheme of things. Some were in awe of a magnificent, colorful celestial sculpture rotating in an infinite field of black. Others saw a frighteningly small, insignificant ball alone in a cold and empty universe. As is true countless times each day in countless ways, it's all about *perspective*.

Perspective can turn molehills into mountains and obstacles into opportunities. For better or worse, It can literally change the world. It just depends on how we look at it. By routinely approaching life from the same perspective, we risk turning the world into an uninspired and predictable place. In the process, it becomes all to easy to overlook even the most obvious or enlightening new information.

Great ideas, ideologies and inventions have happened when people saw things they weren't looking for and discovered things they never expected. Experiencing a fresh perspective is what moves us forward. It can be an eye-opening and sometimes even life-changing adventure.

Whenever we watch a movie, listen to music, read a book, solve a problem or even have a simple discussion with someone, our personal perspectives are challenged. Seeing life through someone else's eyes and considering different points of view are among our greatest and most necessary abilities. On an almost daily basis, incredible advancements in technology allow more and more people, each with their own unique perspective of the world, to communicate alarmingly fast. Our little planet, so majestic and colorful, becomes smaller each day. As a result, our need to acknowledge, tolerate and explore an enormous barrage of new ideas, cultures and points of view is critical.

A photograph allows us to very quickly consider the perspective of the photographer. Unlike a book, movie or song, the photograph can be experienced in an instant. It requires no special skills and virtually no investment of time. It grabs your attention and immediately involves you in its message.

    This collection of photos is an exercise in perspectives. It celebrates fleeting moments and everyday objects, the kinds of things we generally take for granted. It offers revealing perspectives on many things we may never have believed had anything to reveal. Even minutiae can become monumental depending on how we look at it

    These photos were taken with a Nikon D70 Digital SLR camera and most have earned recognition in international online photo contests. Some may be more surprising than others, some may inspire and some may just be entertaining. I've tried to make them compelling and I hope you find at least a few of them memorable. However you view them, I hope you'll enjoy them and that they encourage you to step outside your routine perspective and try on a different set of eyes.

- Dan Holm

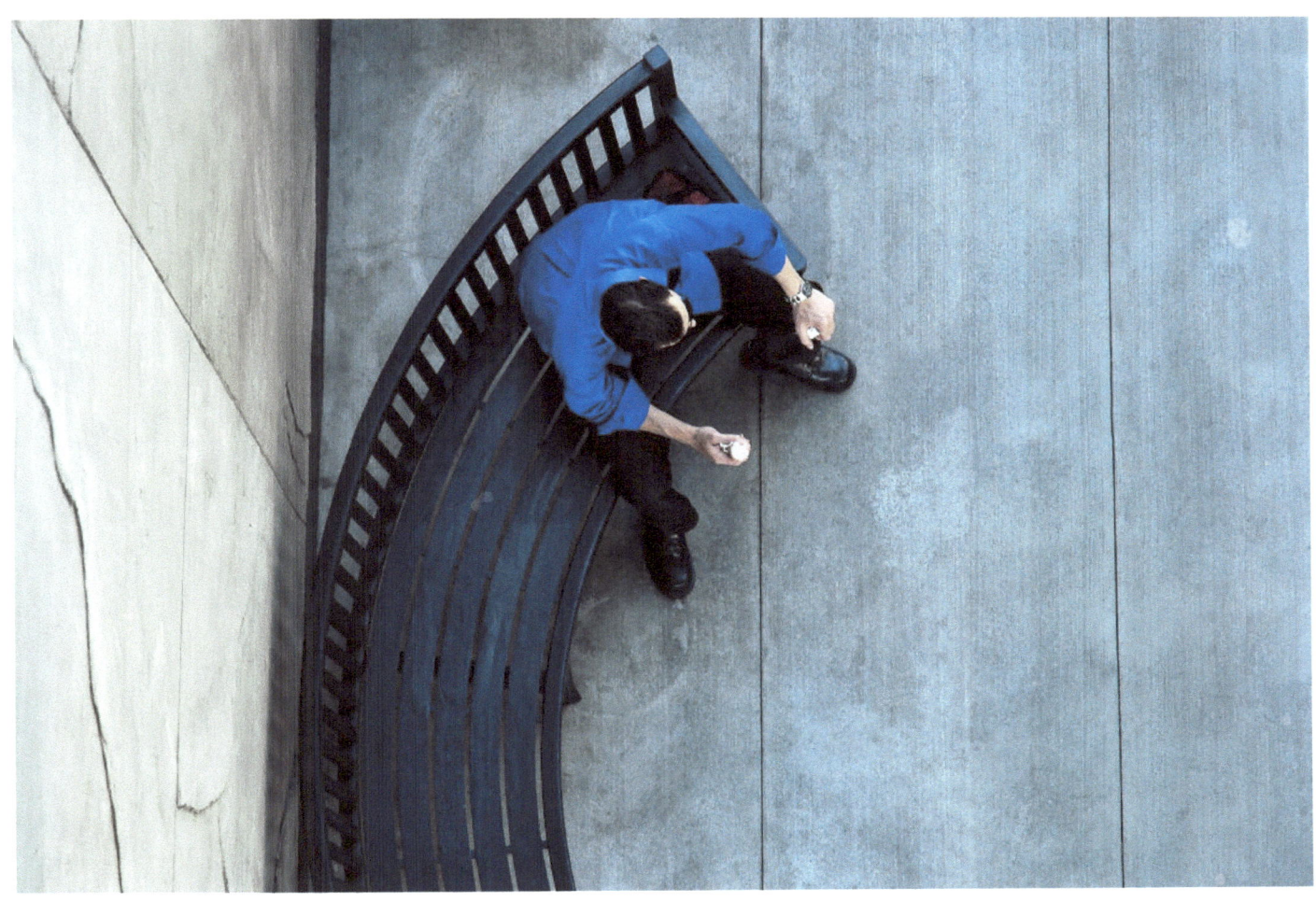

Along The Wall

The picture wasn't complete until he became part of it.

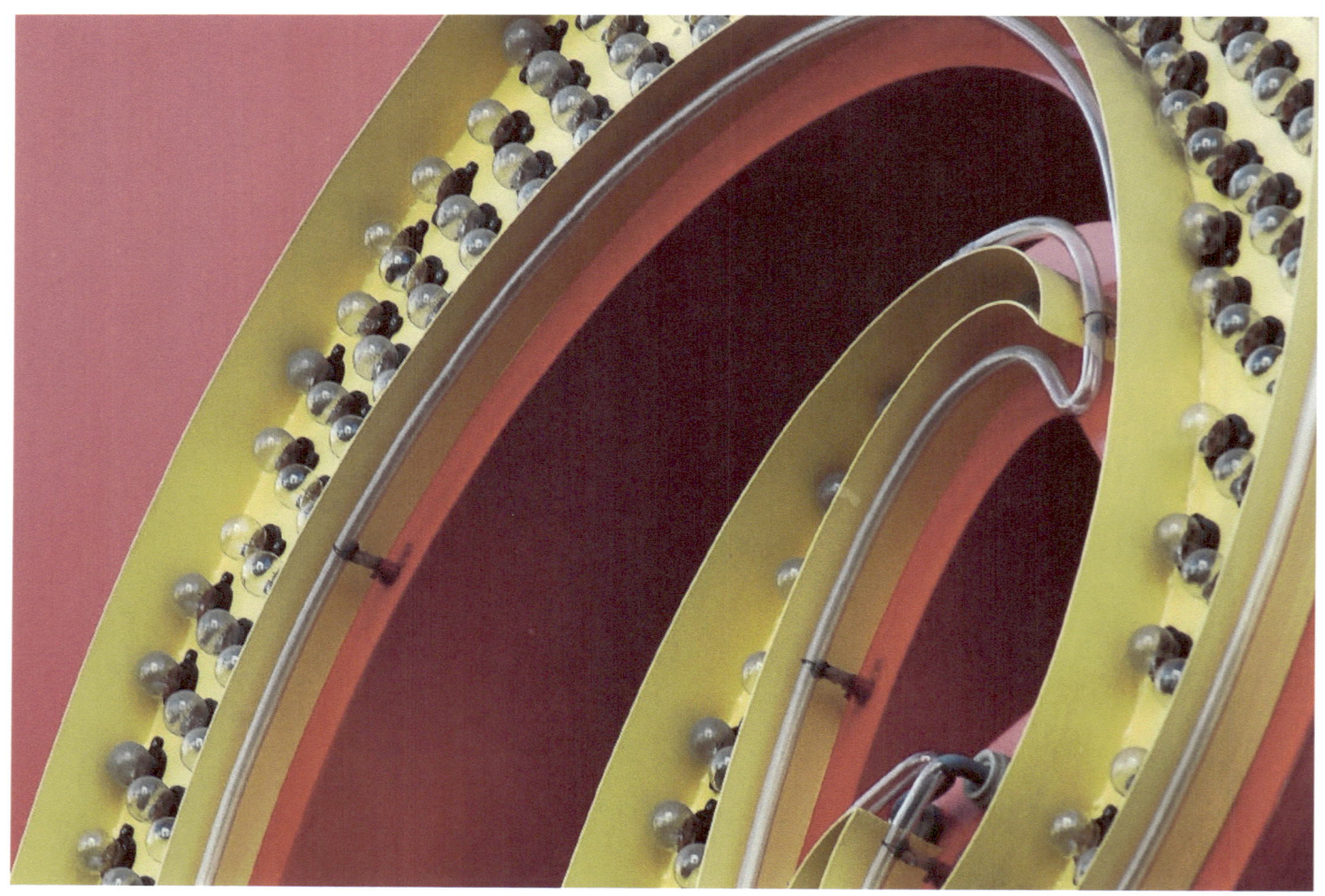

It's A Sign

I looked up and knew immediately that it was a sign.

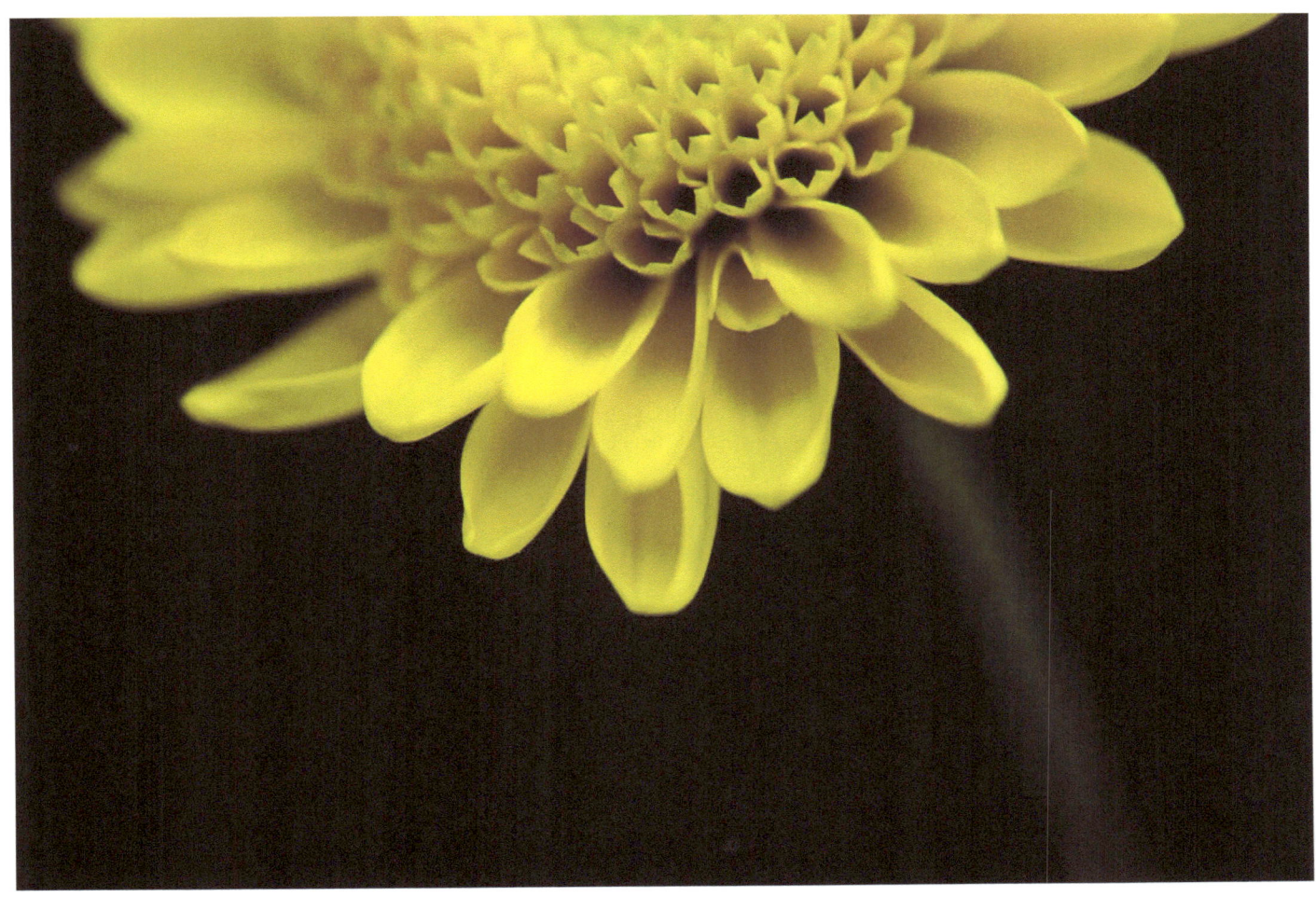

In Part

A part can be just as dynamic as the whole.

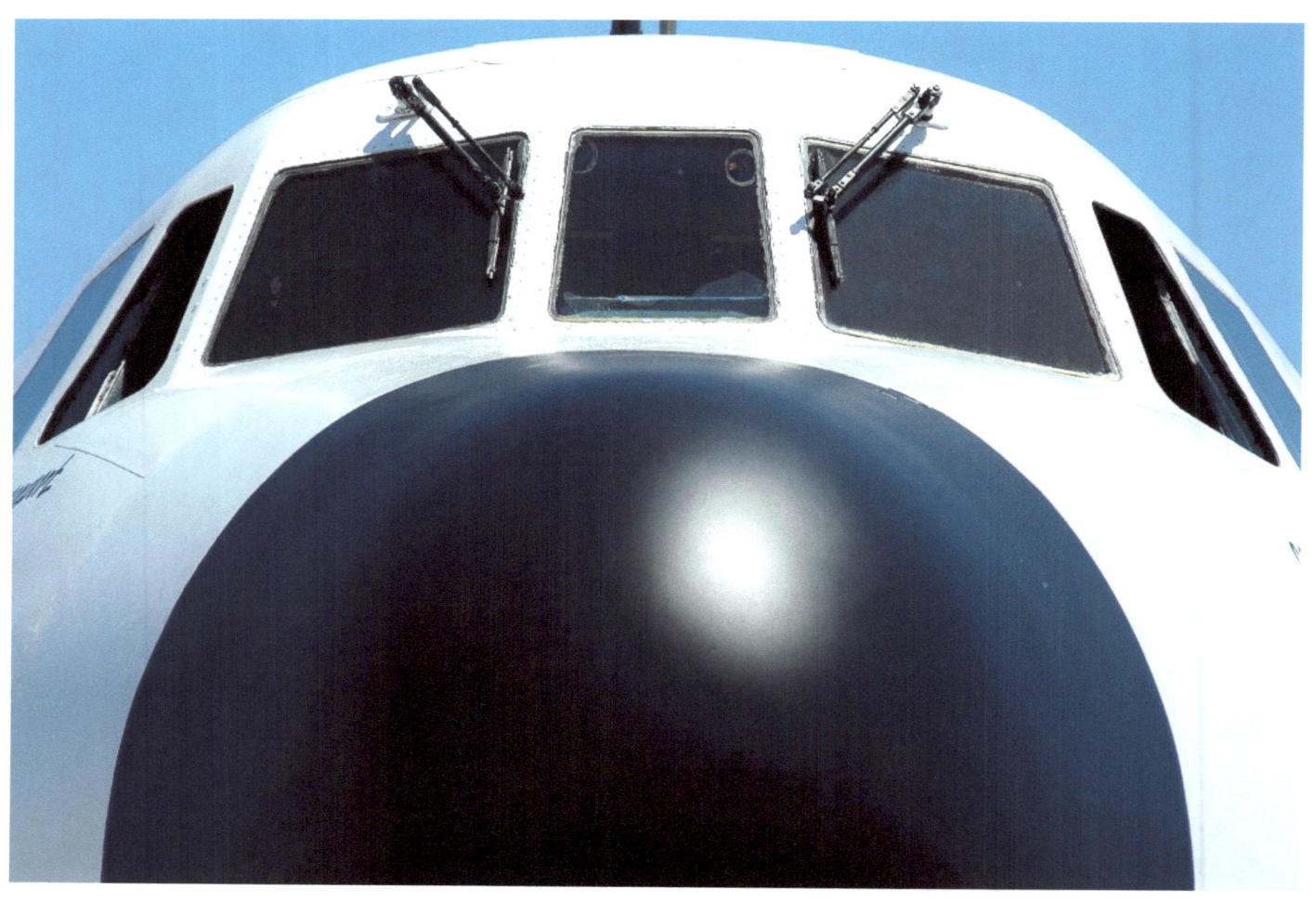

By The Nose

Follow the nose; it usually gets there first.

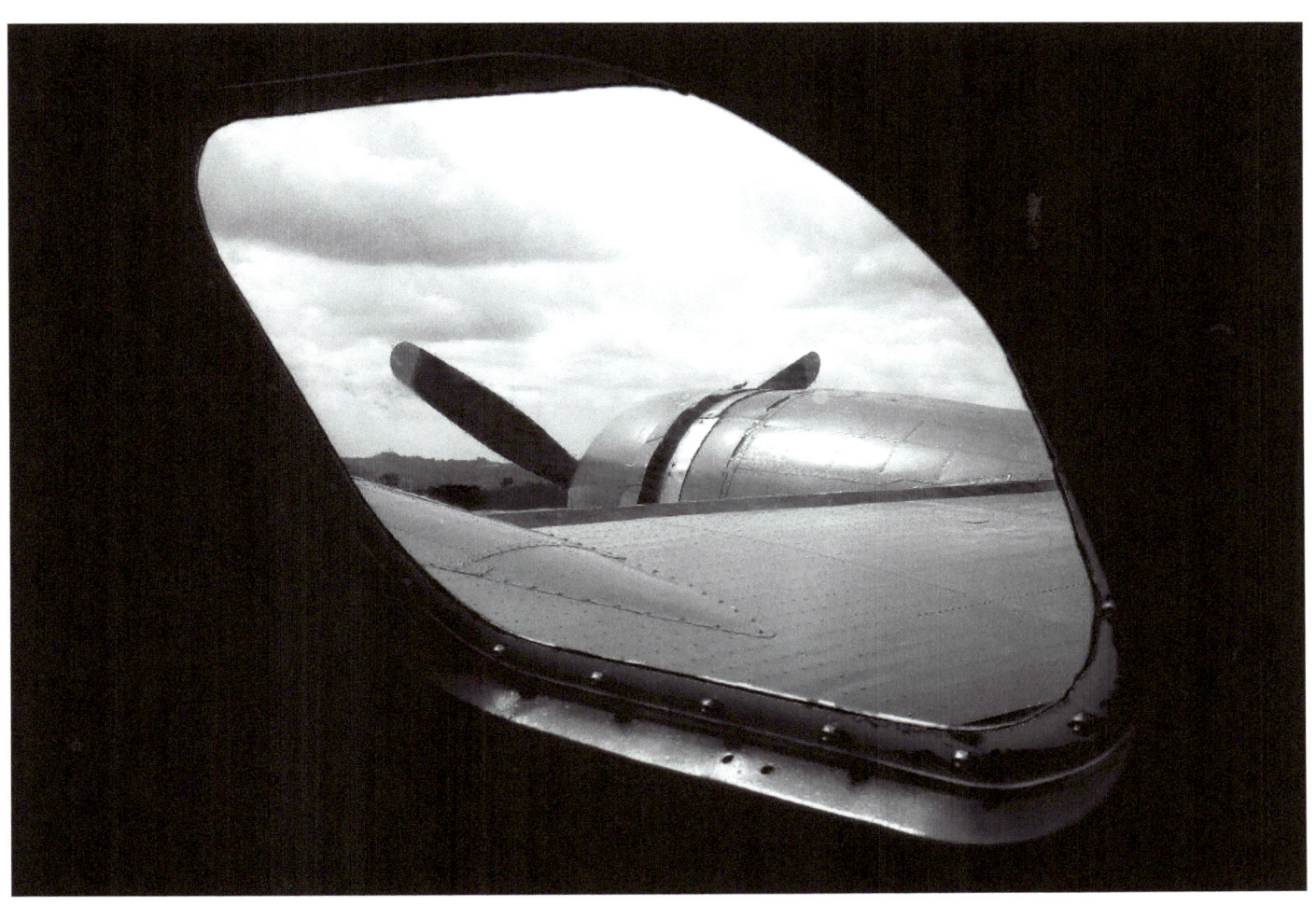

Wing And Window

Once the engine starts, the sky's the limit.

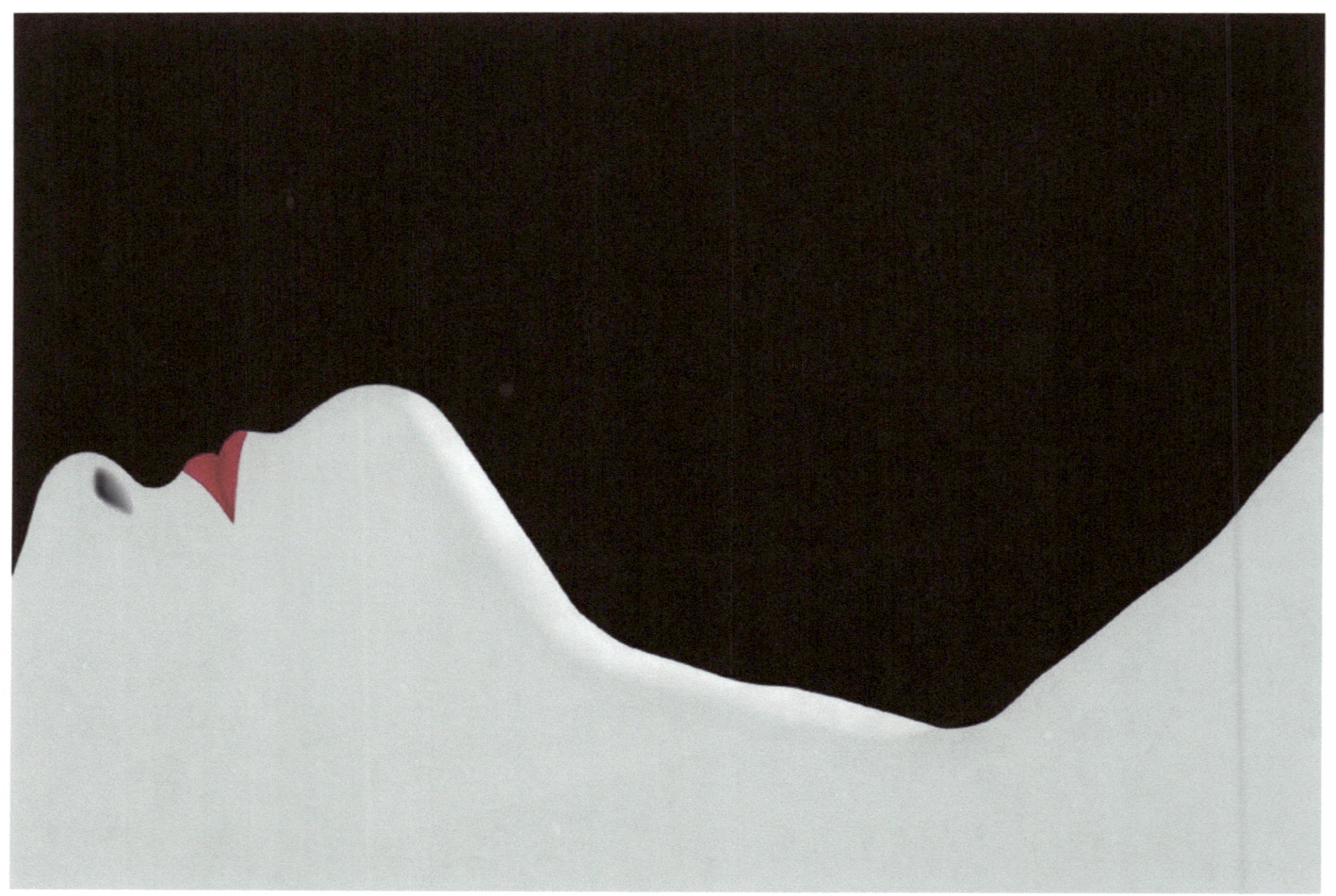

Contours

The right perspective turns common contours into an evocative landscape.

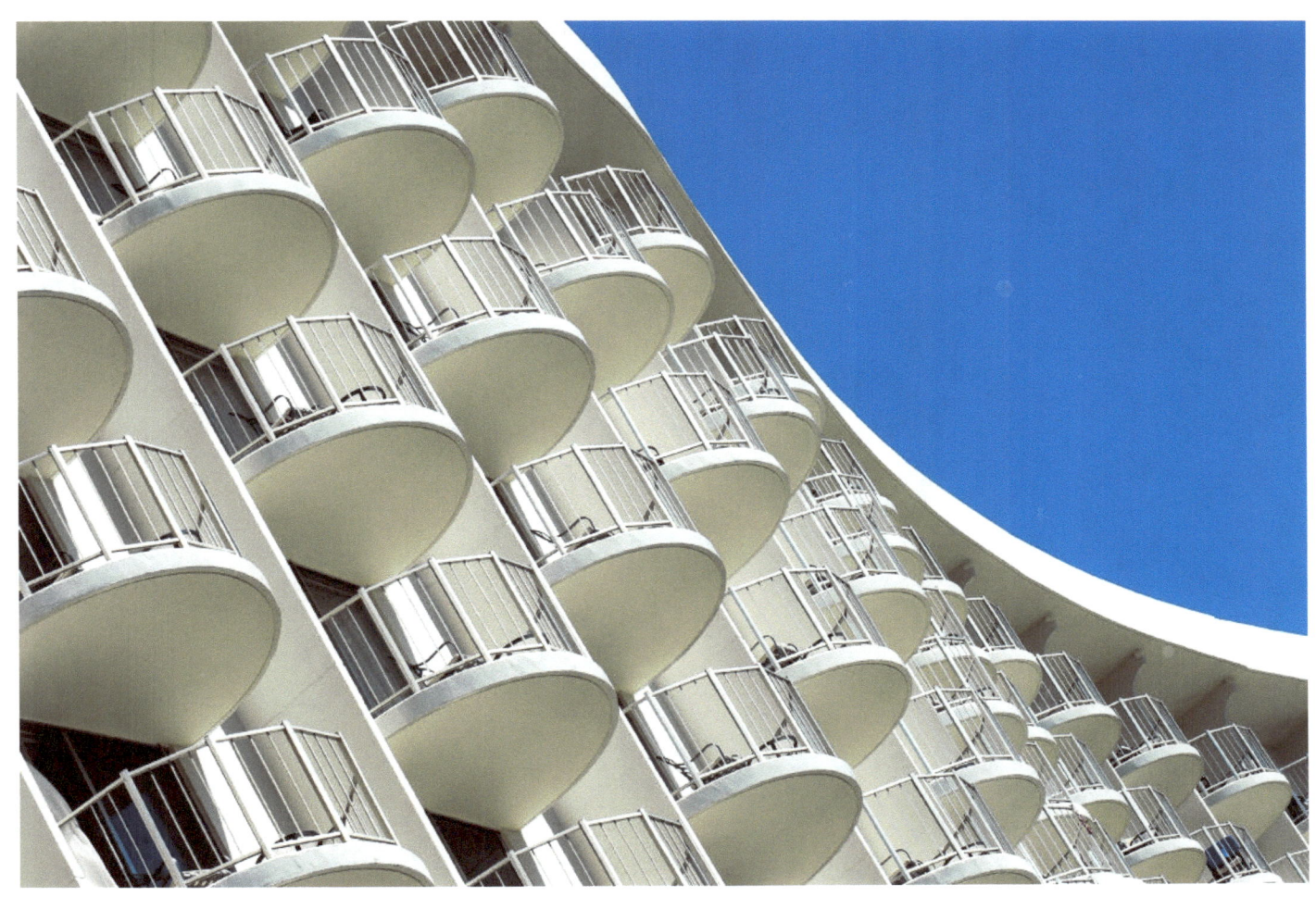

Balconies And Blue

A dramatic angle reveals elegant motion and dynamic life in concrete and steel.

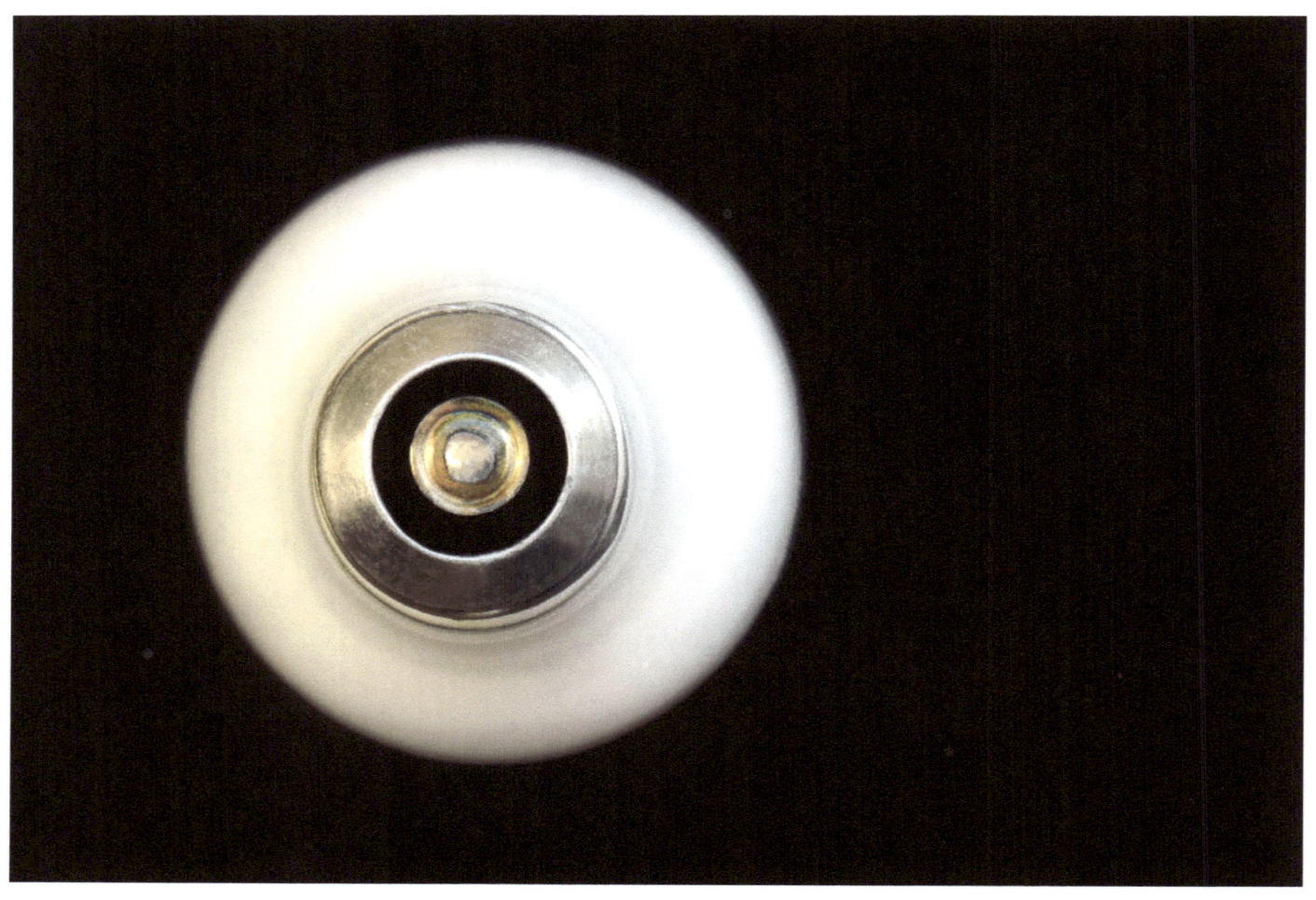

Bright Idea

An idea turned upside down becomes an entirely different concept.

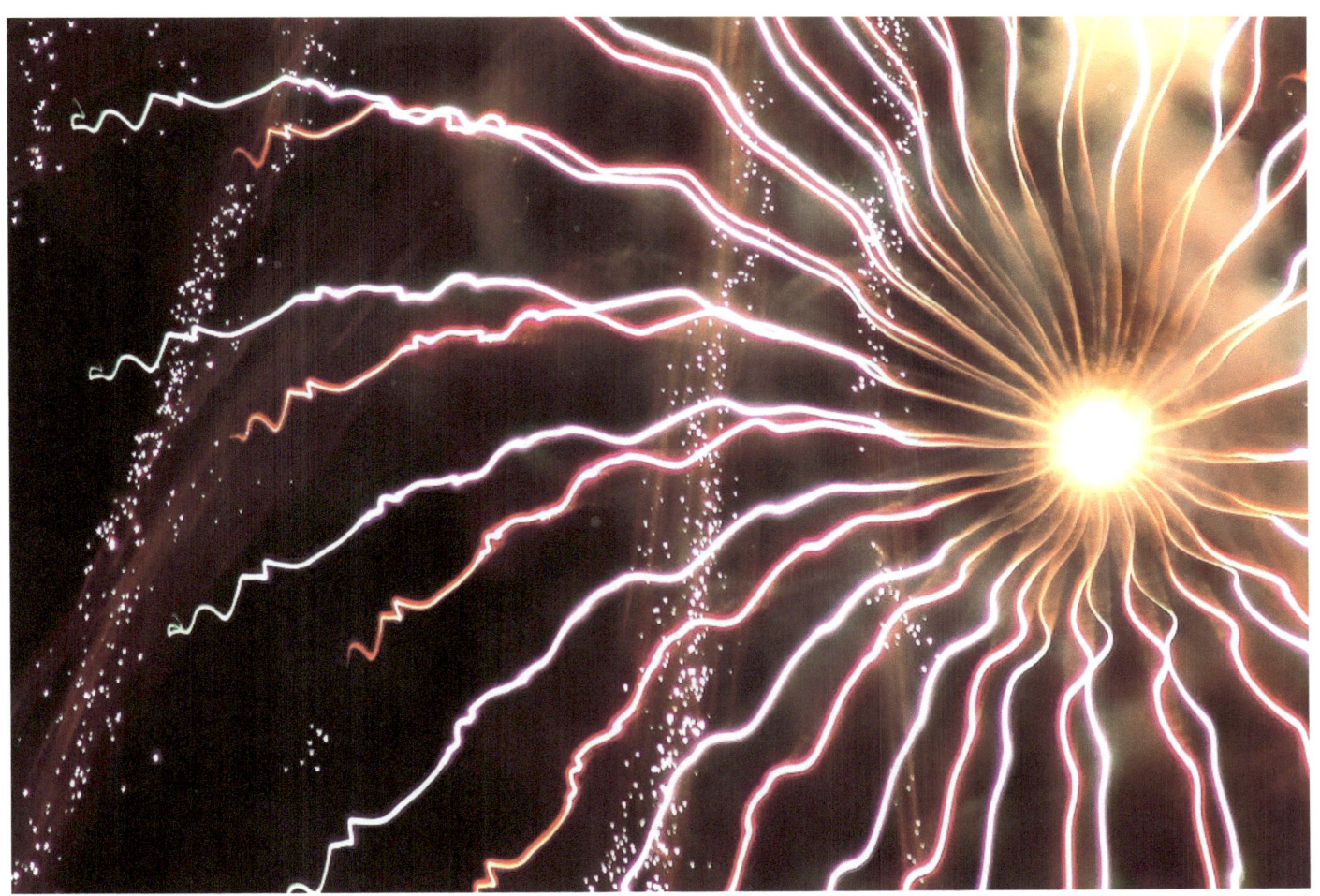

Nova

Deep space drama takes shape overhead in a slow shutter fireworks shot.

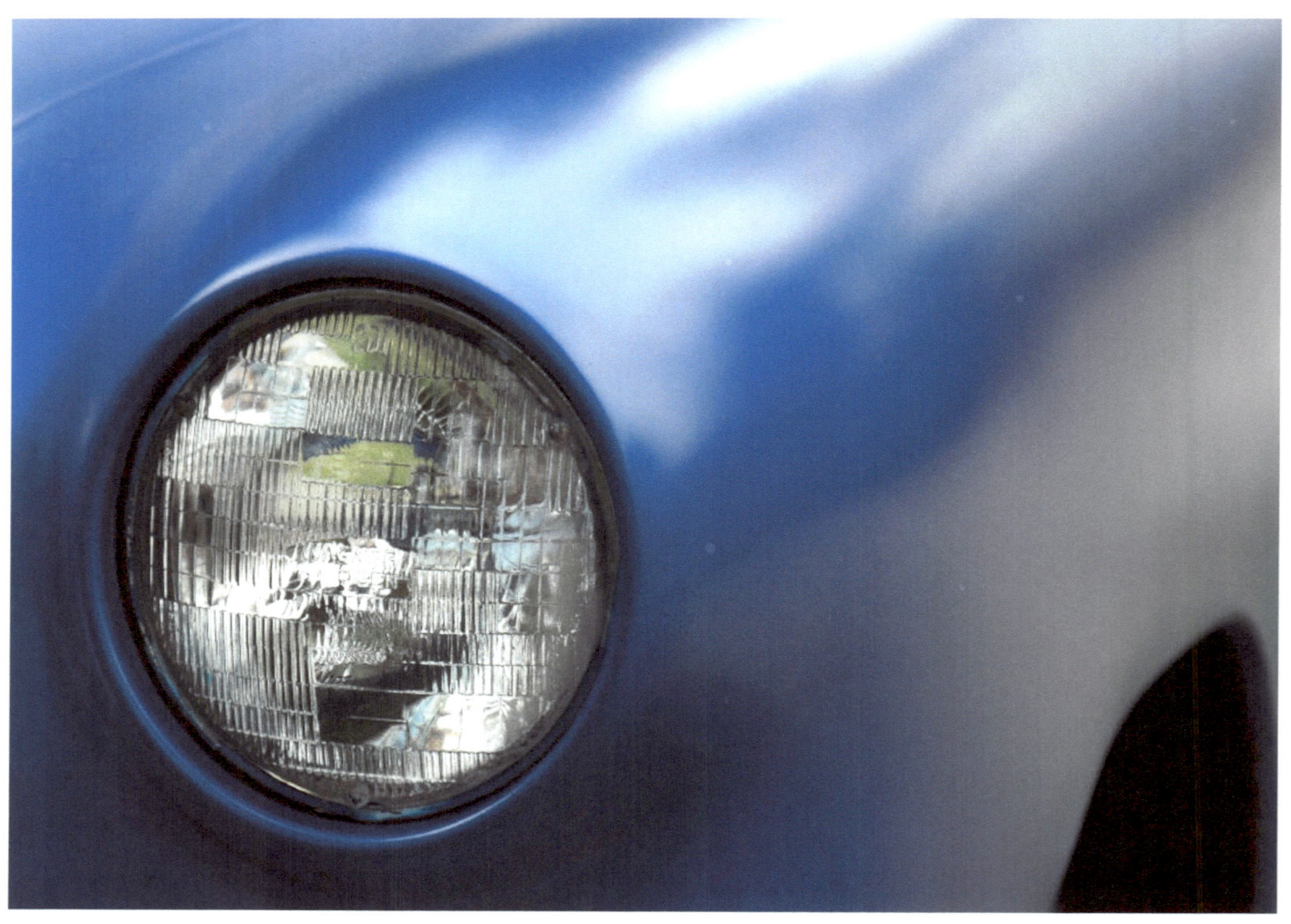

Out Of The Blue

From out of the blue, one unwavering eye focused on the horizon.

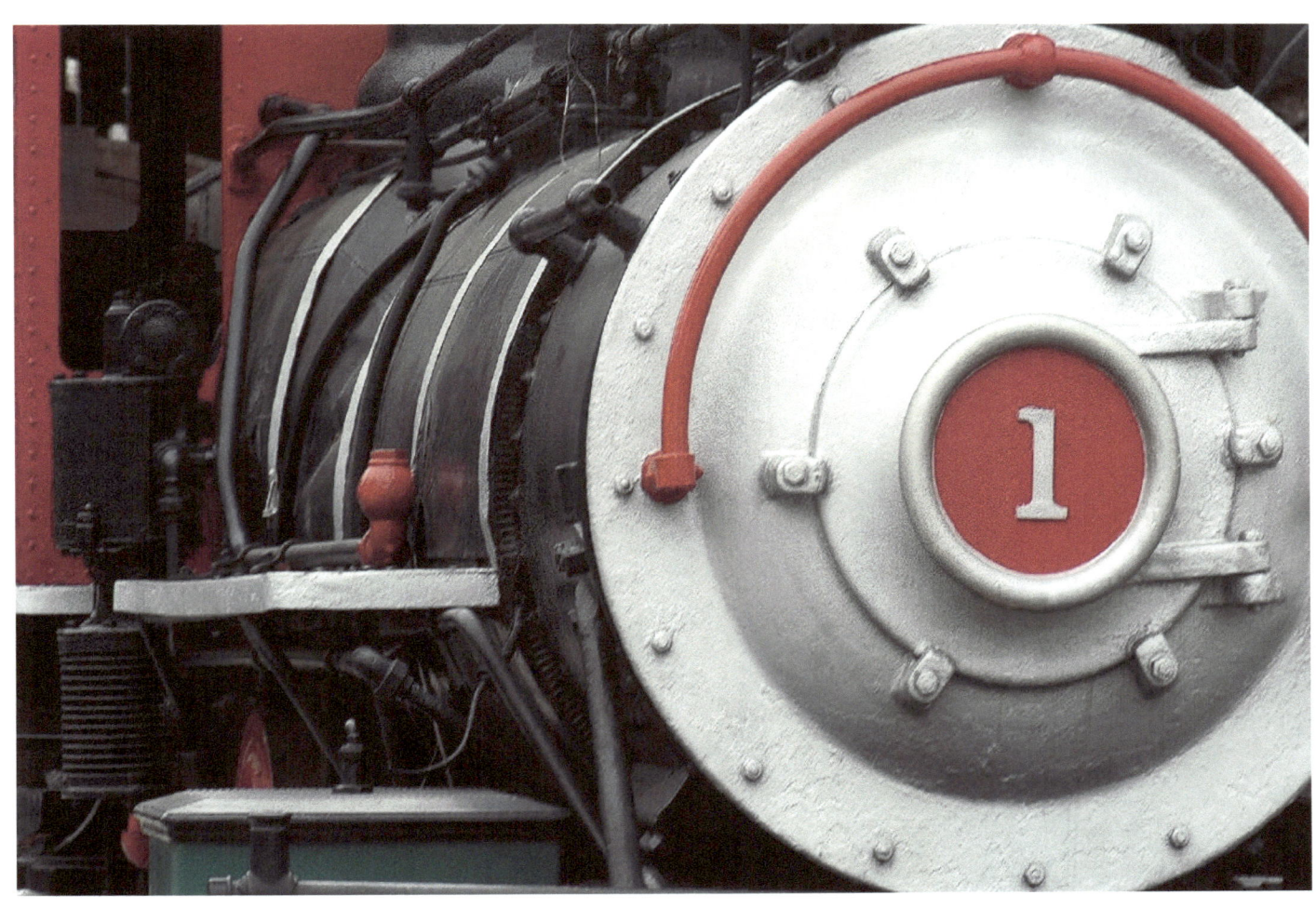

Number One

They say there's only one number one but I have a feeling there's a number of other ones out there.

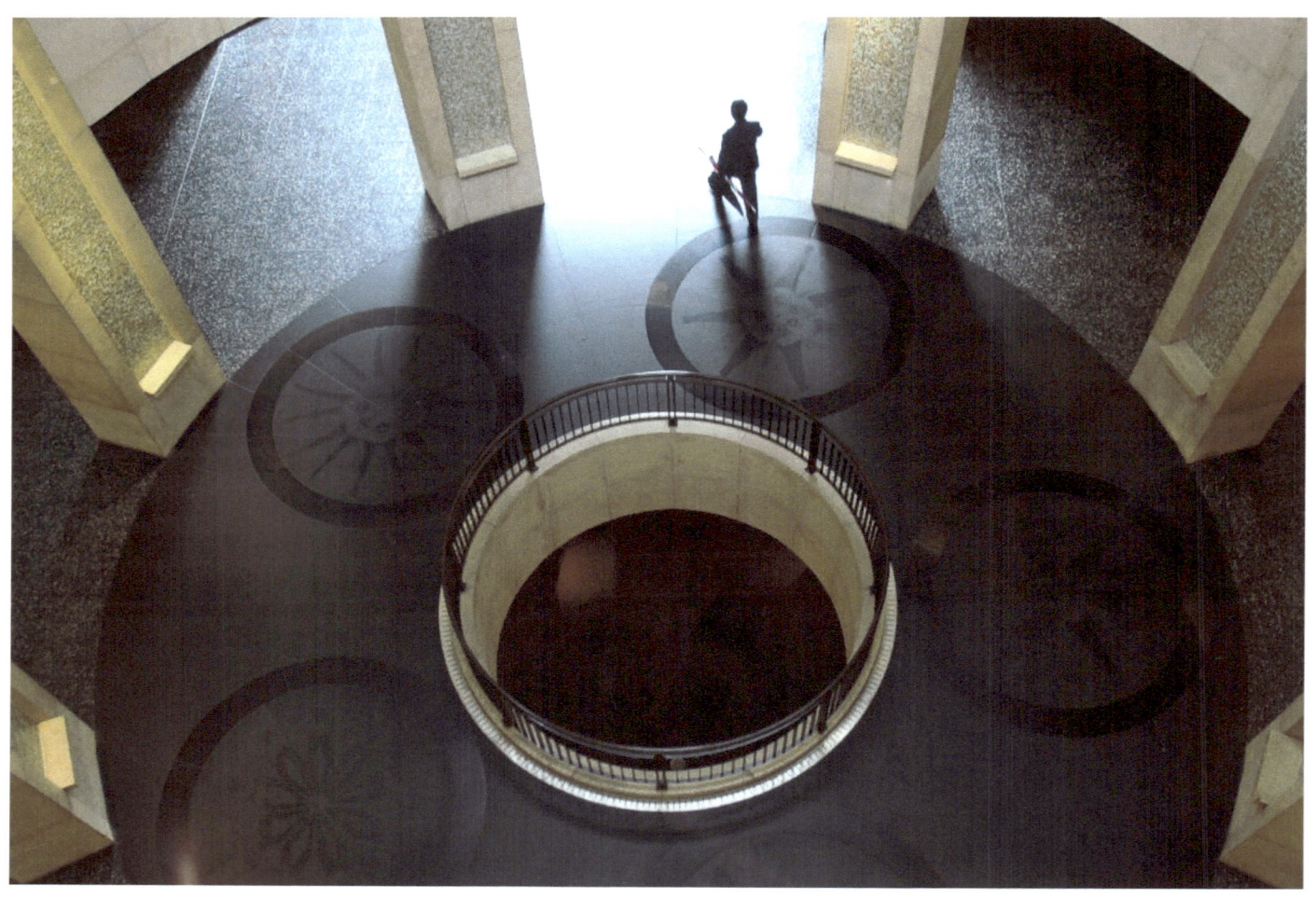

Inner Circle

An inside look at the inner circle.

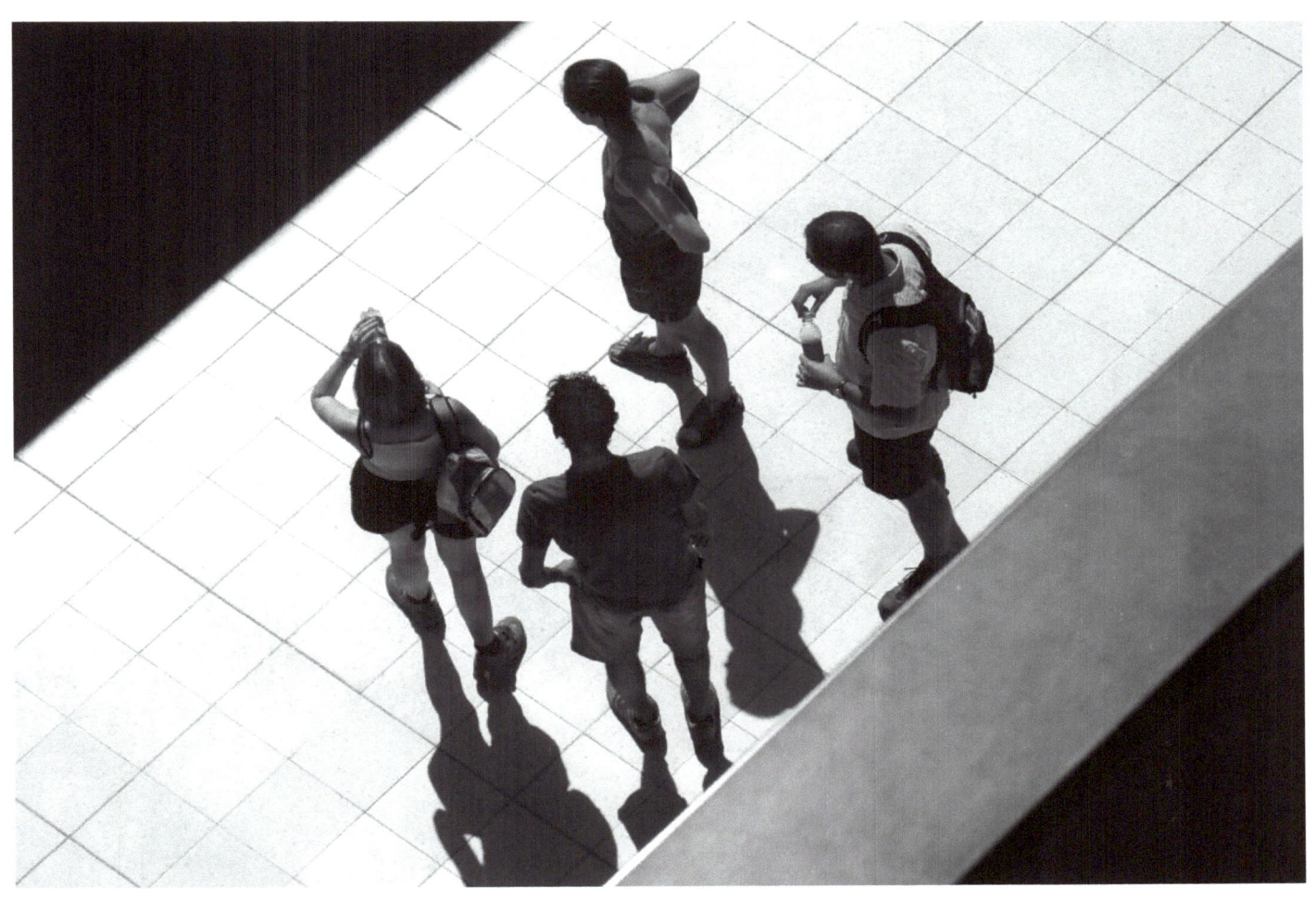

Group Regroup

They stopped to decide where to go next. All they knew for sure was that they'd get there together. That's what friends do.

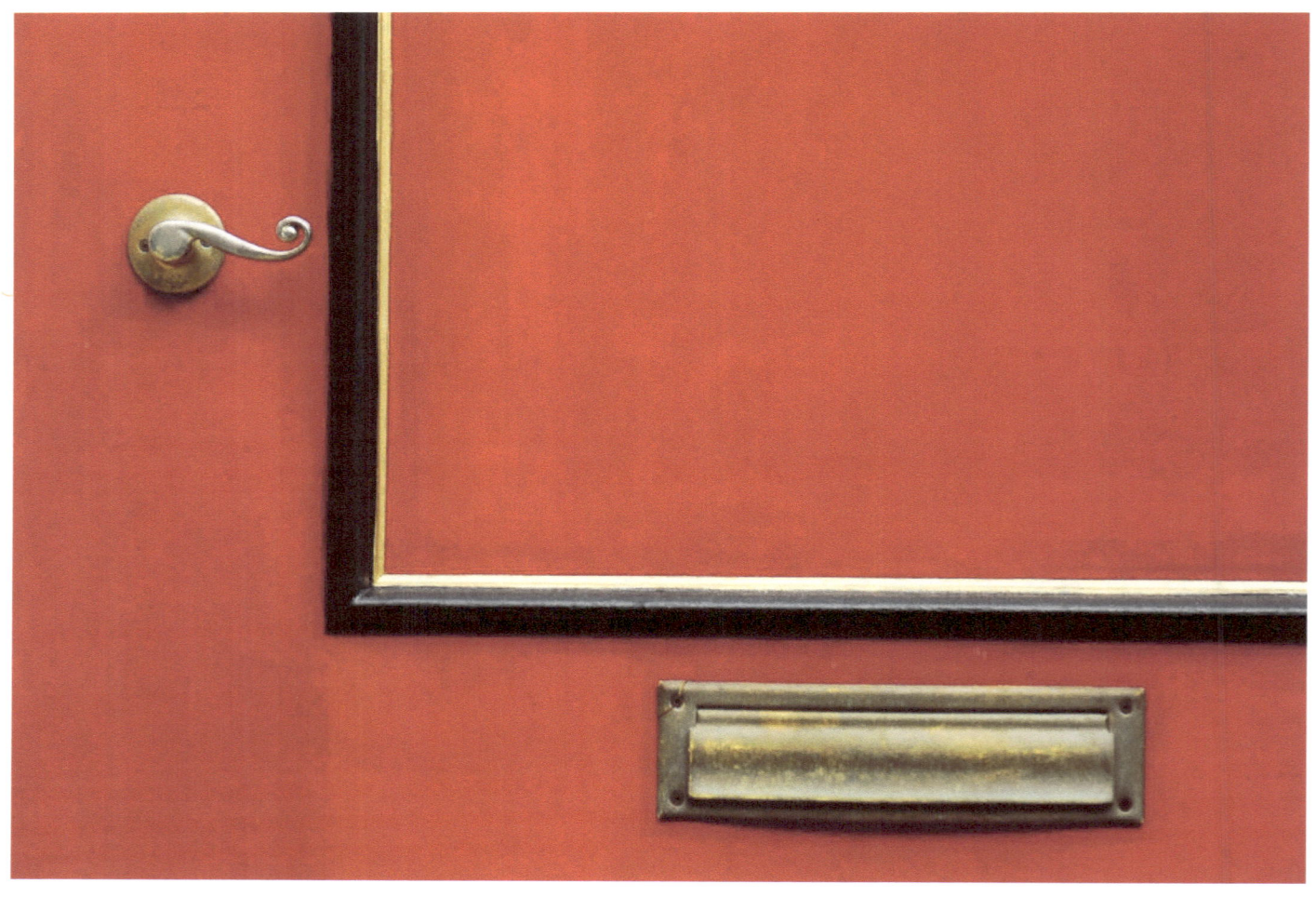

This Red Door

A few simple shapes turn this plain red door into a striking design.

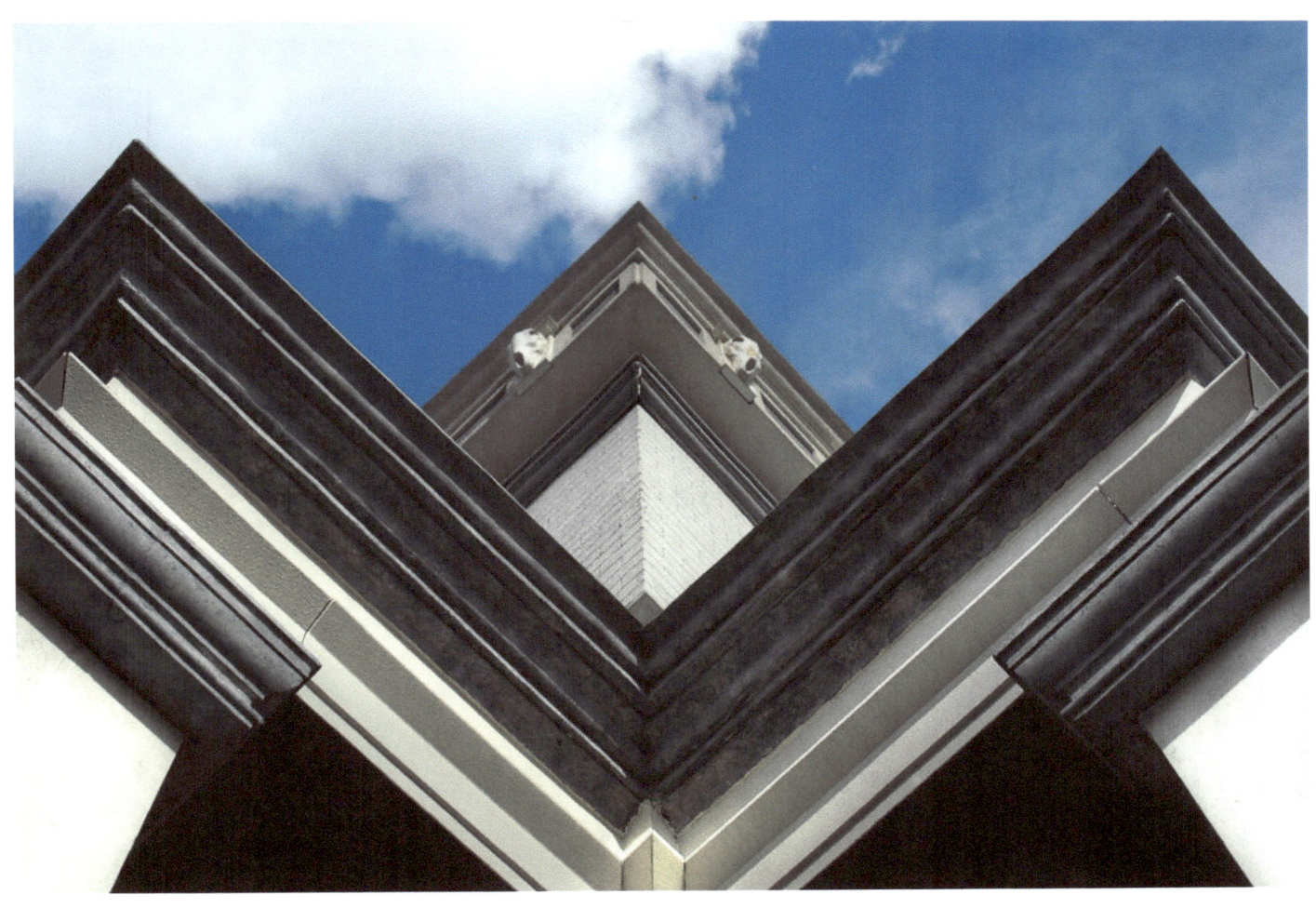

Drama Overhead

There's a whole new world overhead filled with color, framed with drama.

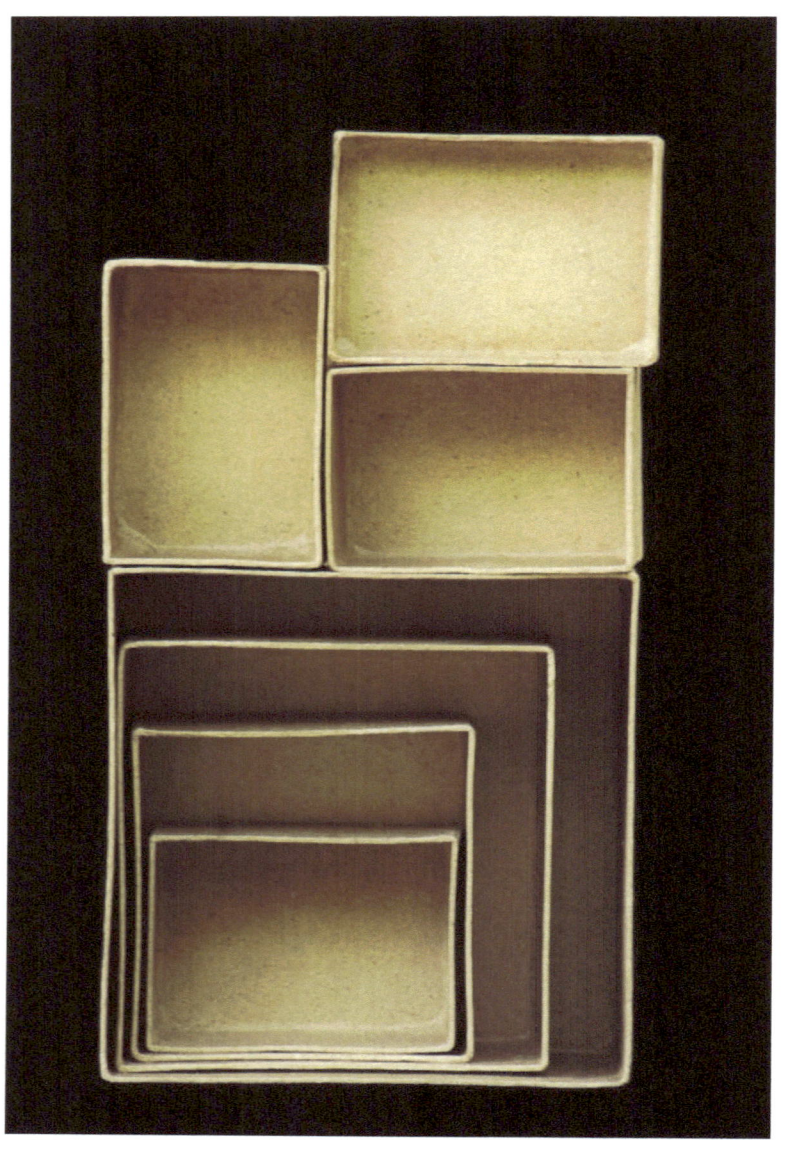

Organizational Chart

Organization happens when the pieces fit.

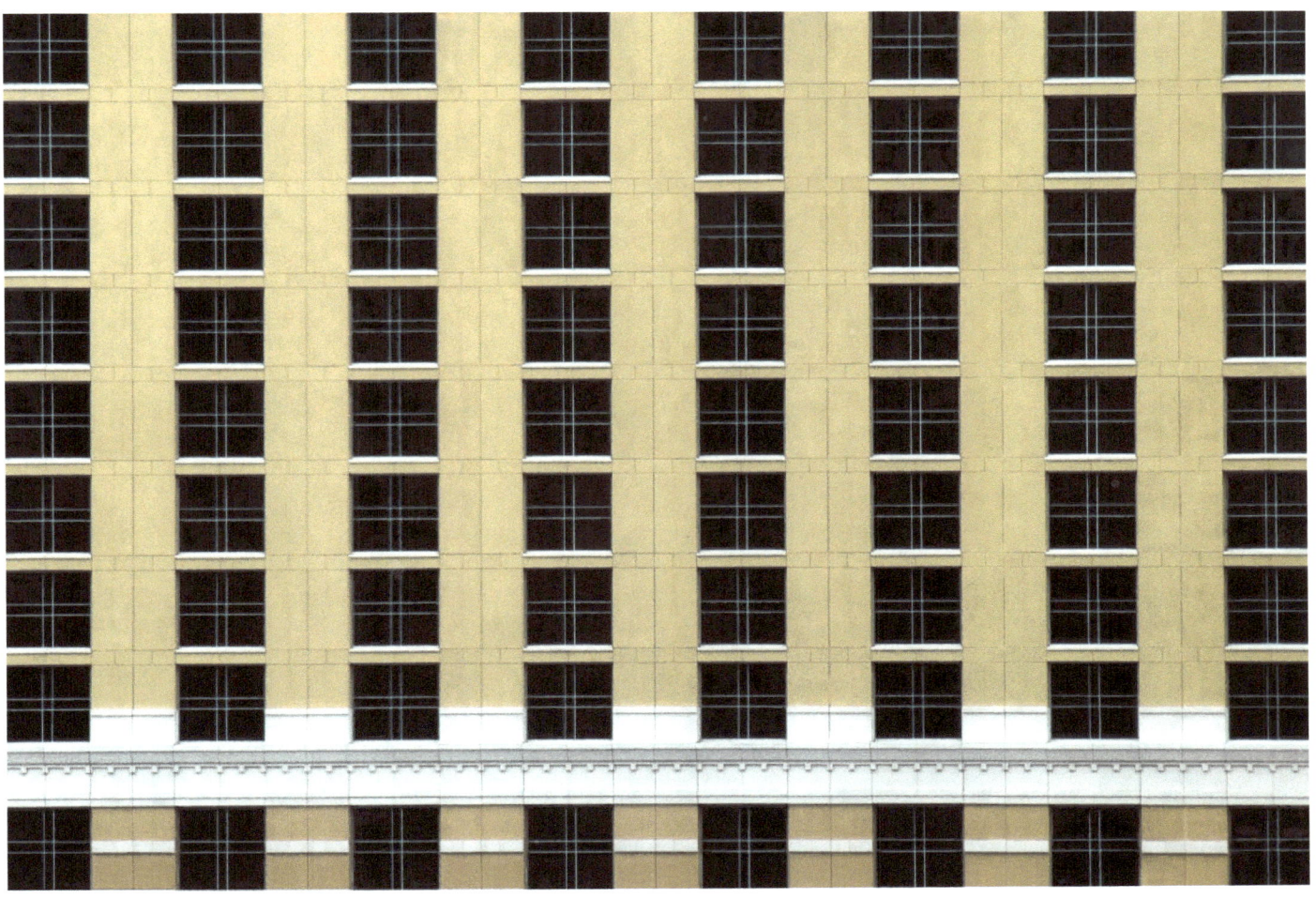

Floors

Floors above, floors below. The building is all about floors.

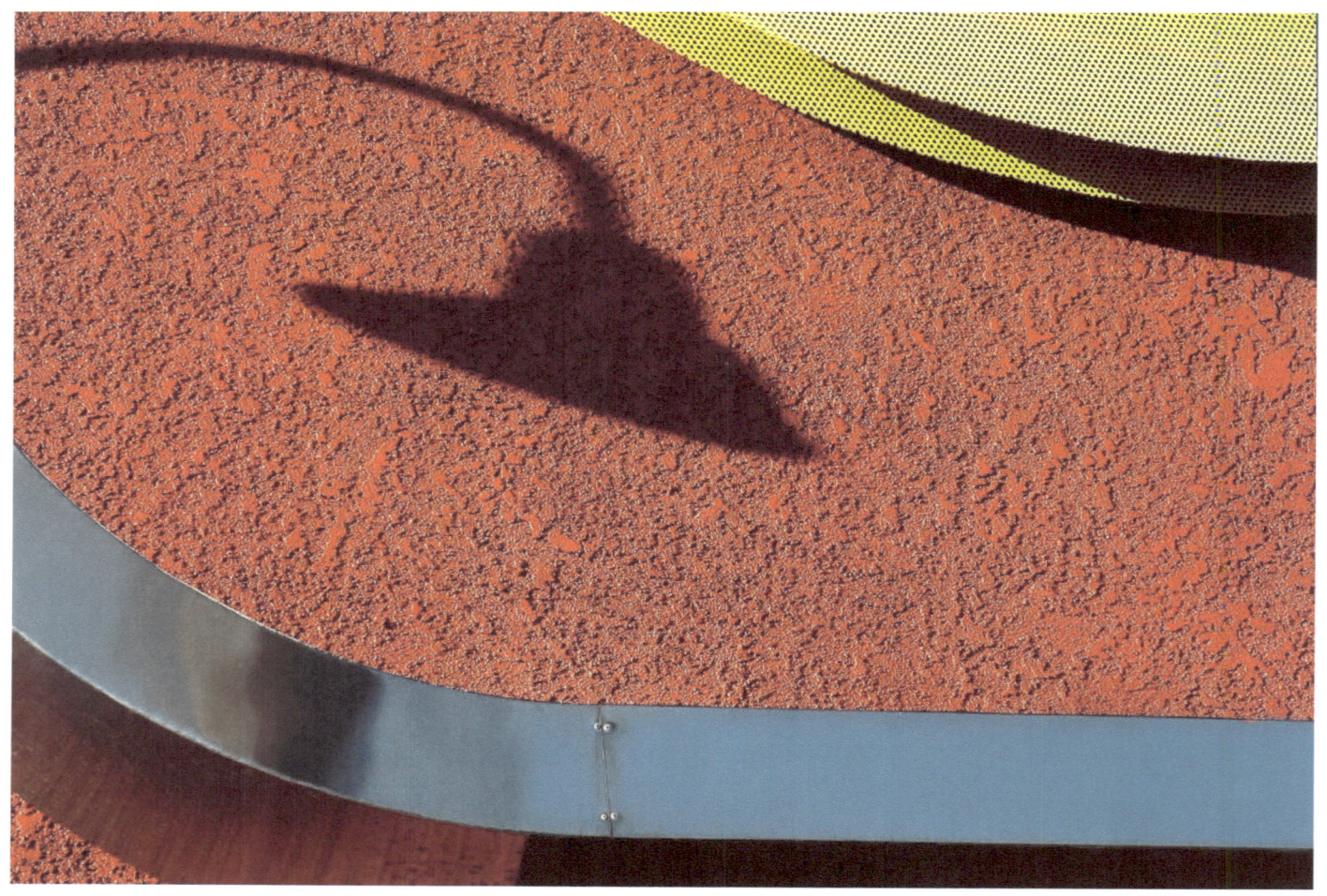

Light Shadow

On the way to sunset, a light shadow made a fleeting impression.

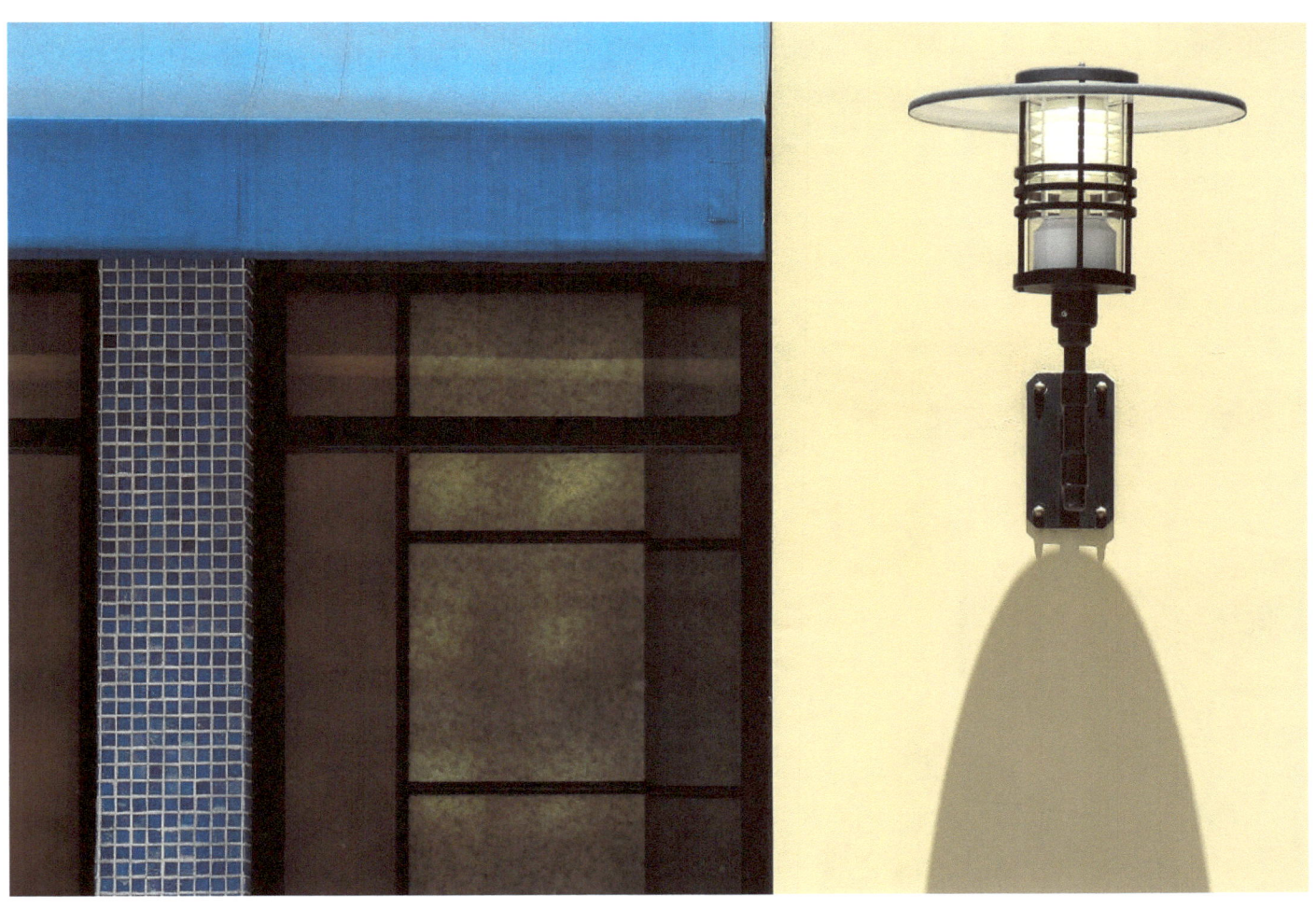

Around The Corner

Shadows stretch and light bounces right around noon, right around the corner.

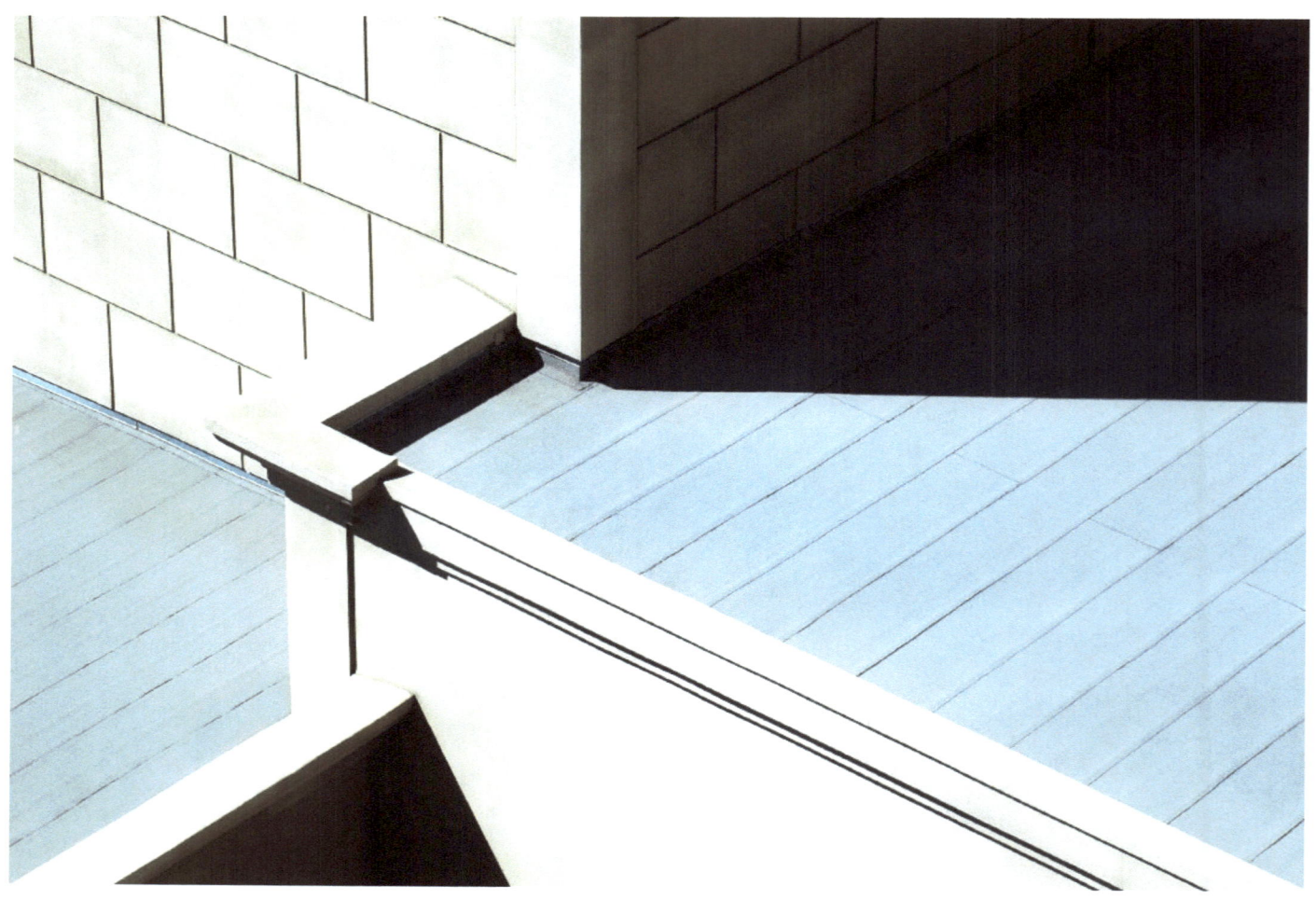

Always An Angle

In the right light, it becomes obvious; there's always an angle.

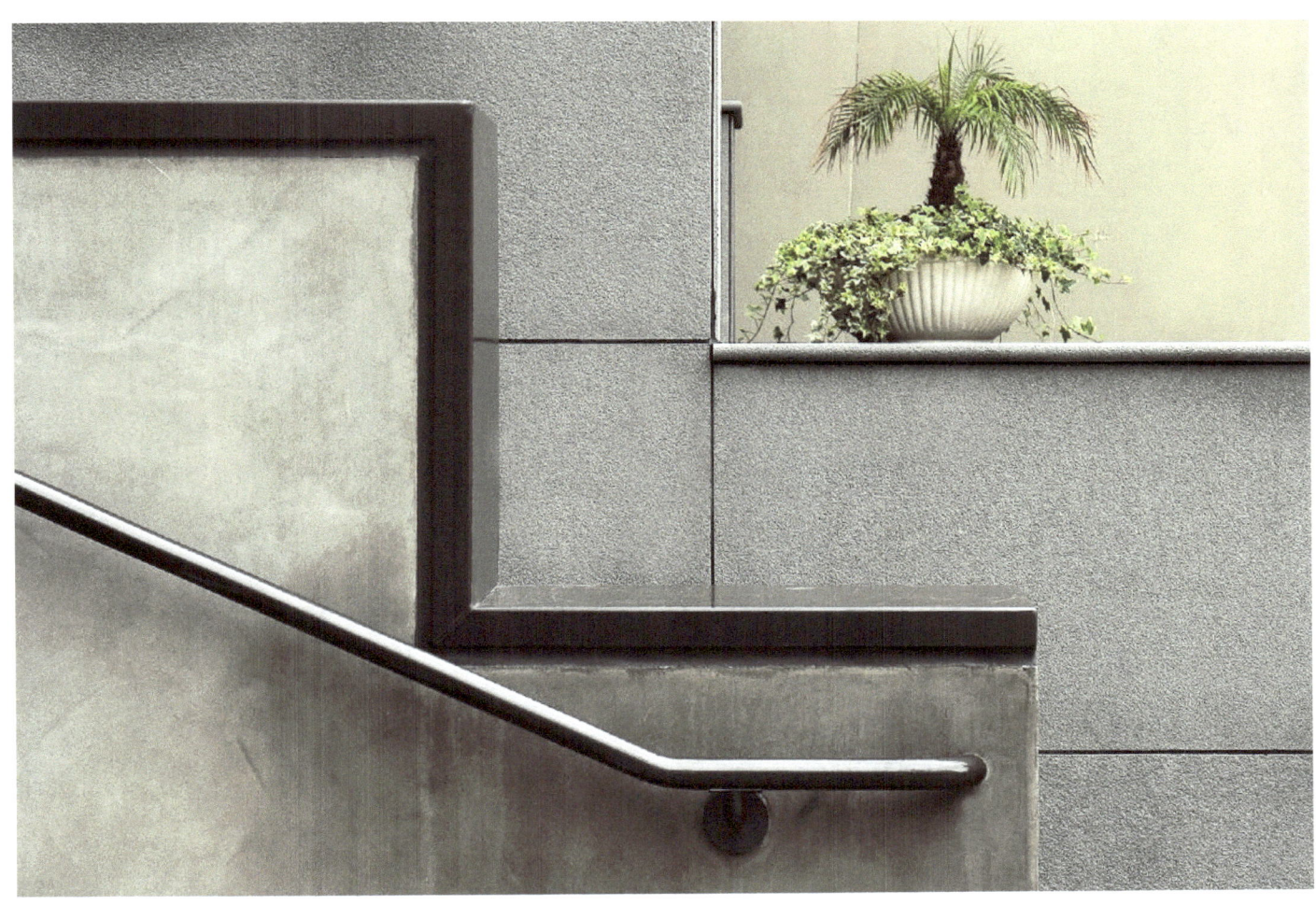

Framed

Layers and lines fall into place, framing a picture within the picture.

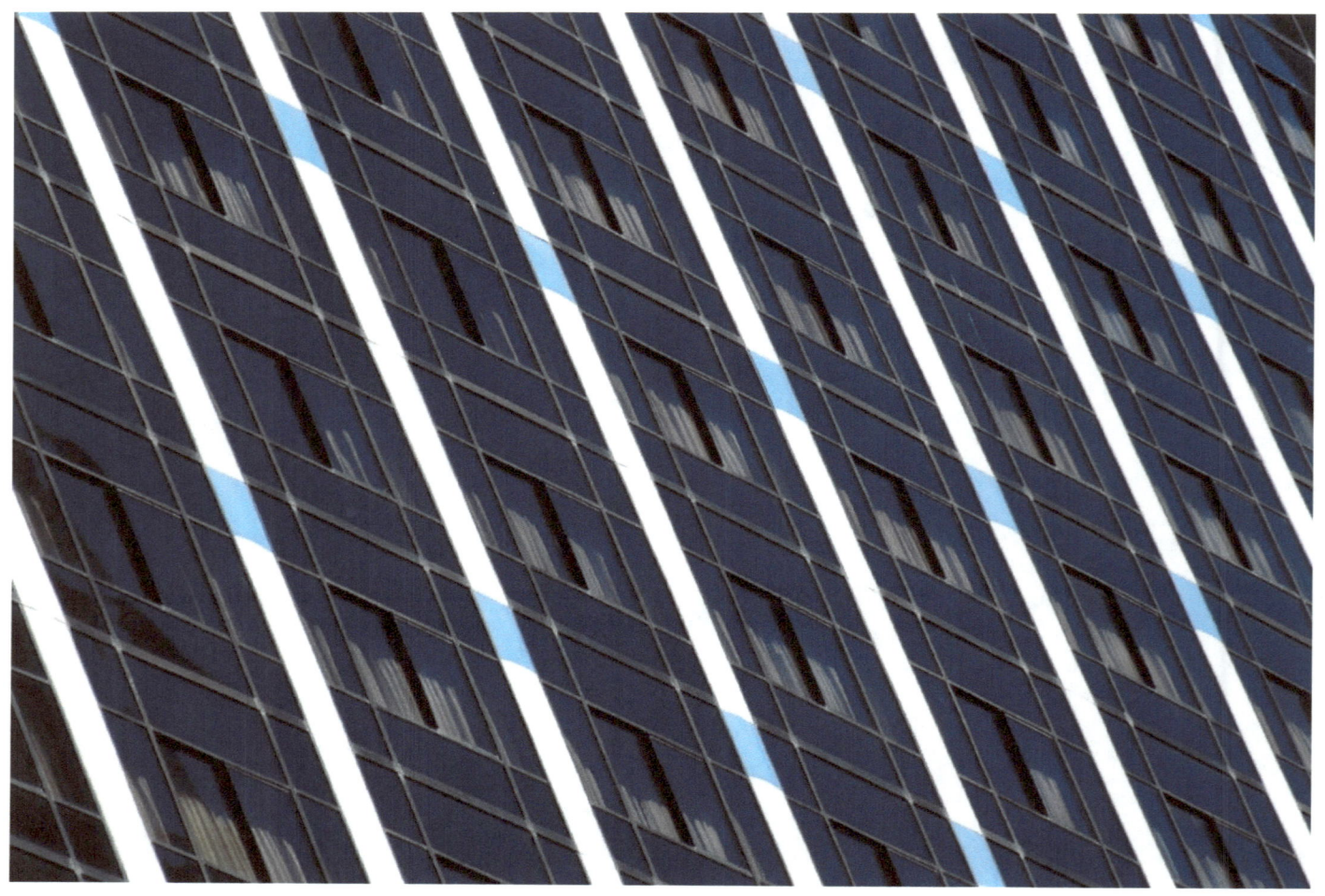

Stripes

Living between the lines, they'll never see the pattern unless they step outside.

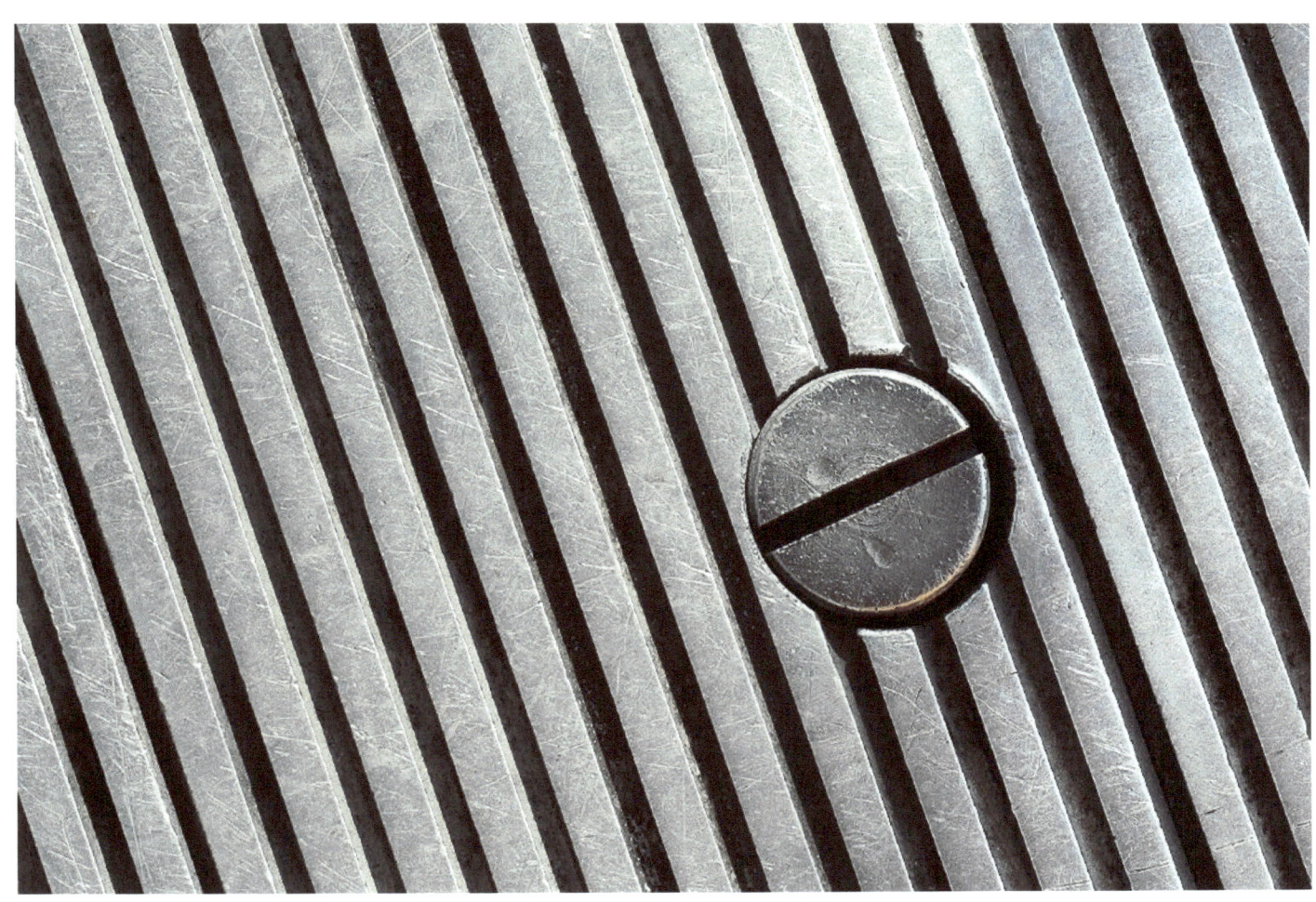

The Opposition

A circle among lines, a diagonal against diagonals. The opposition is the center of attention.

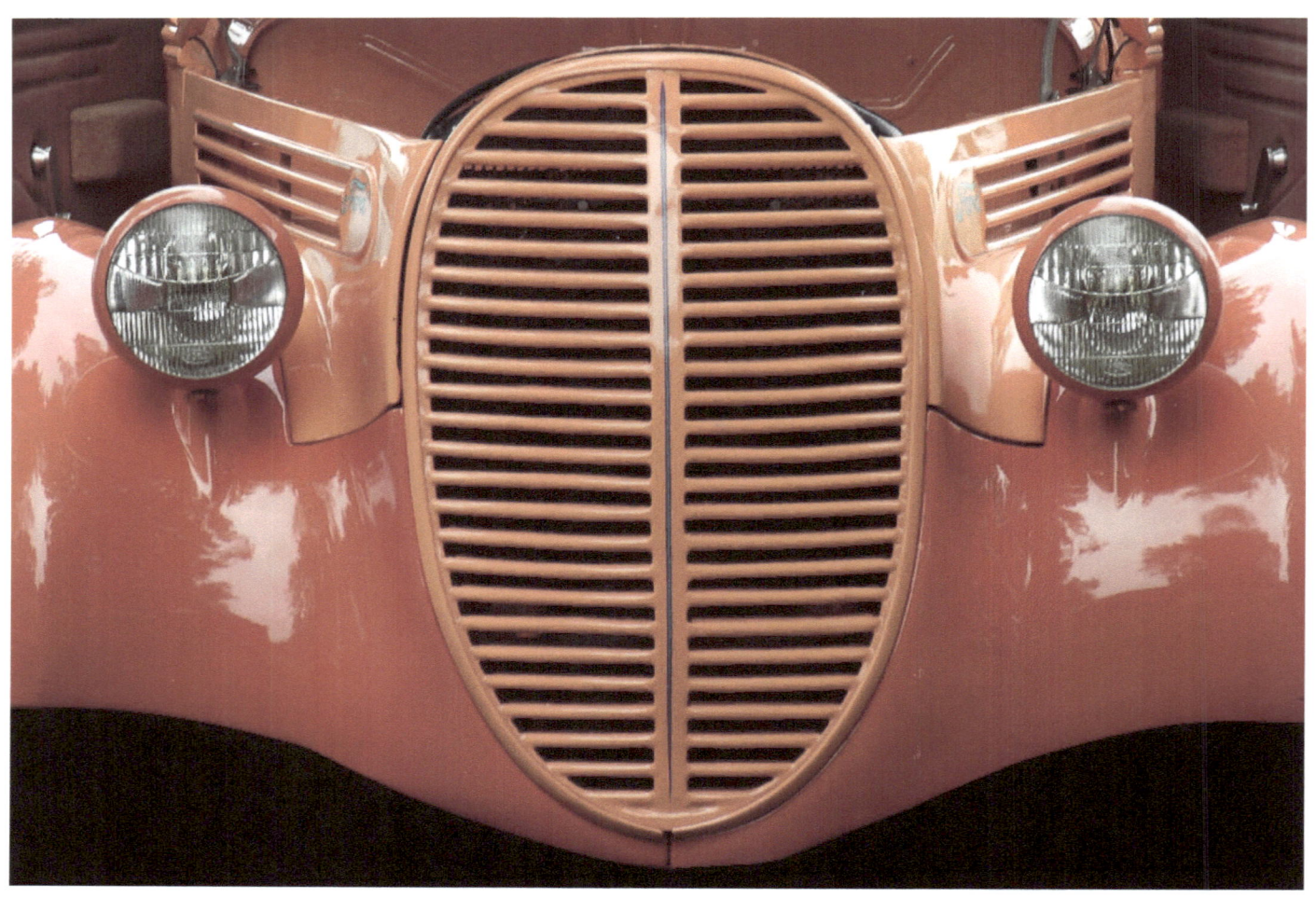

Startled Car

Red faced, wide-eyed and open-mouthed, the camera caught this blushing car by surprise.

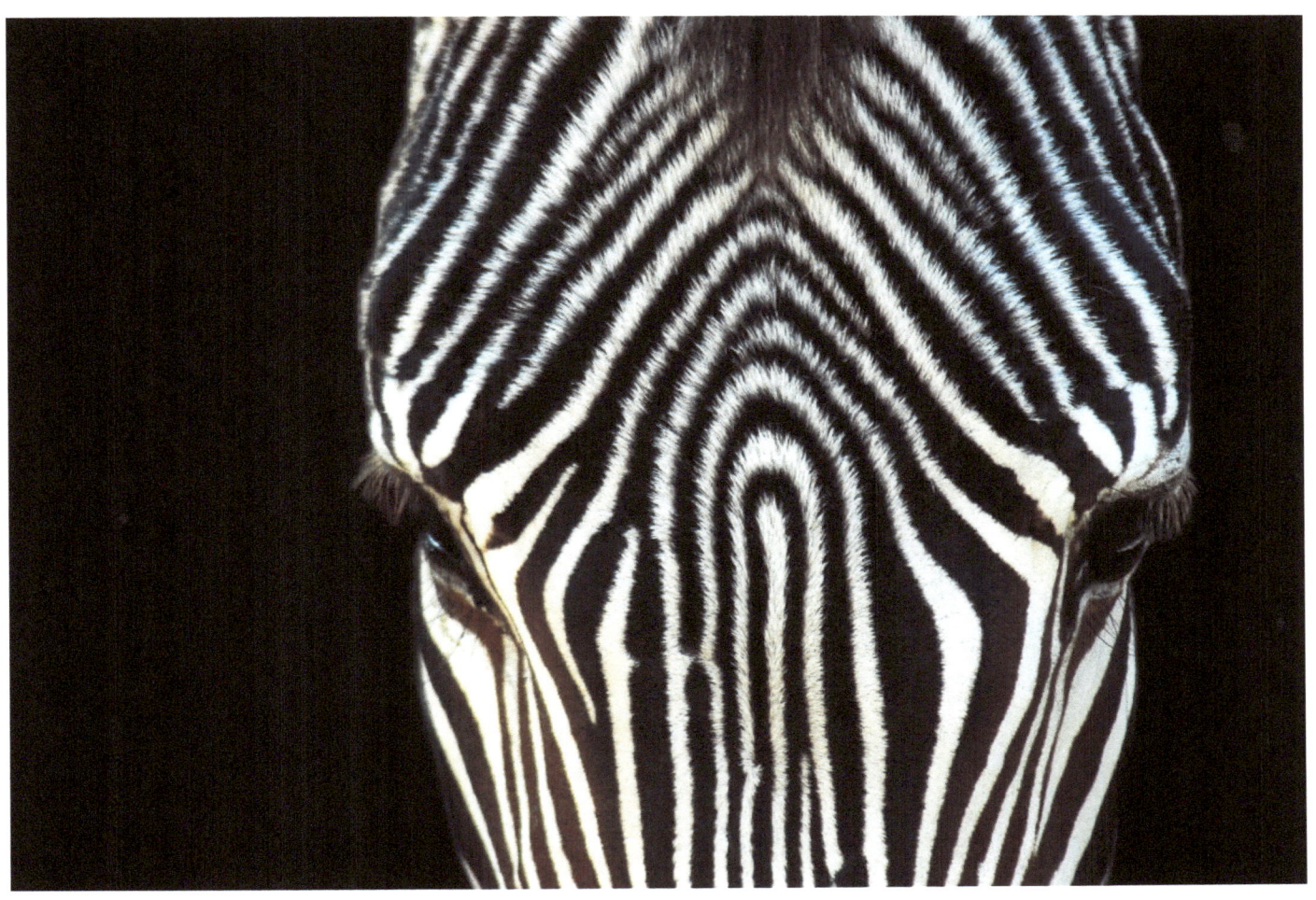

Animal Print

Patterns inside of patterns inside of patterns.

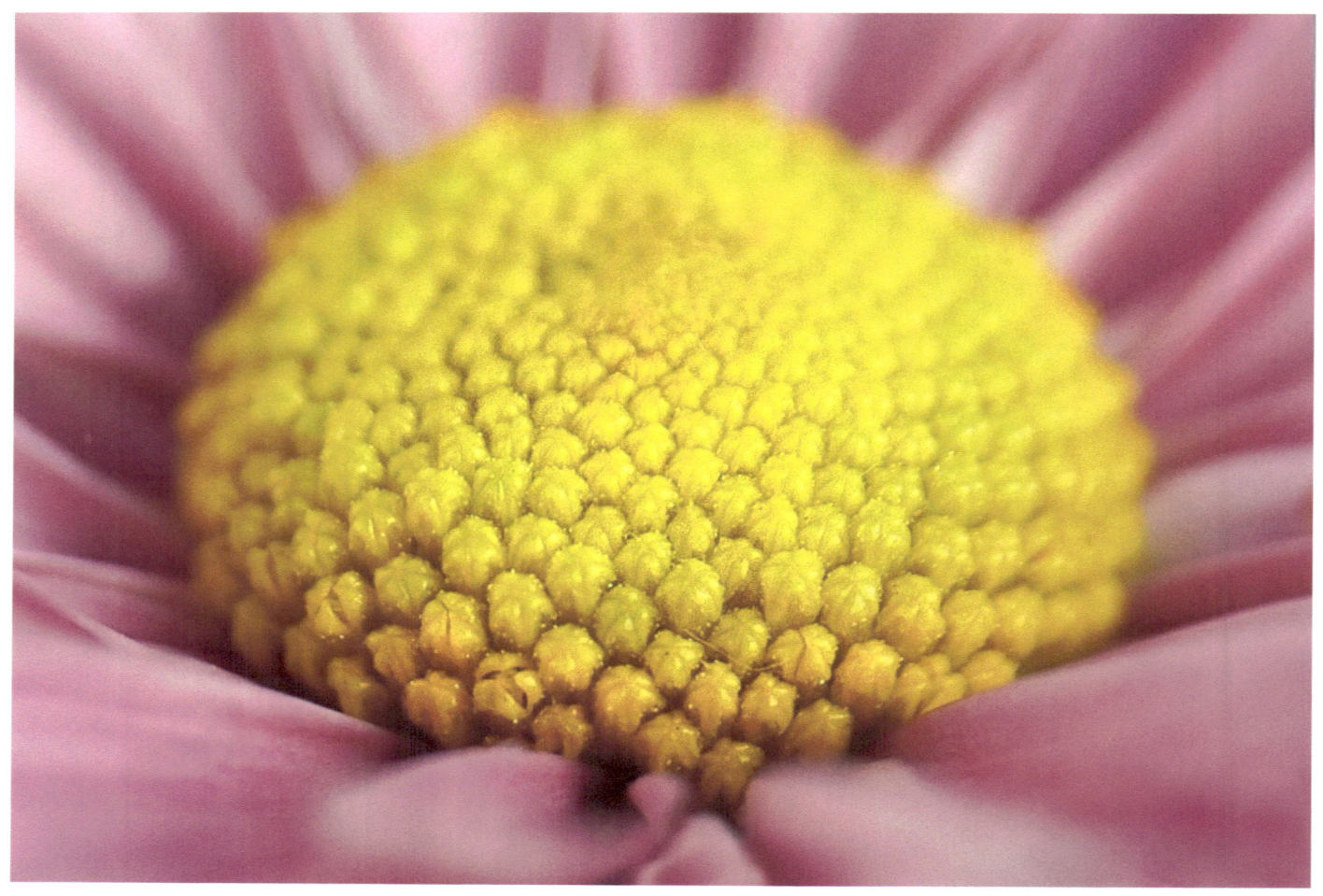

Crown Jewels

On a velvet cushion, the shining center of the flower presents itself.

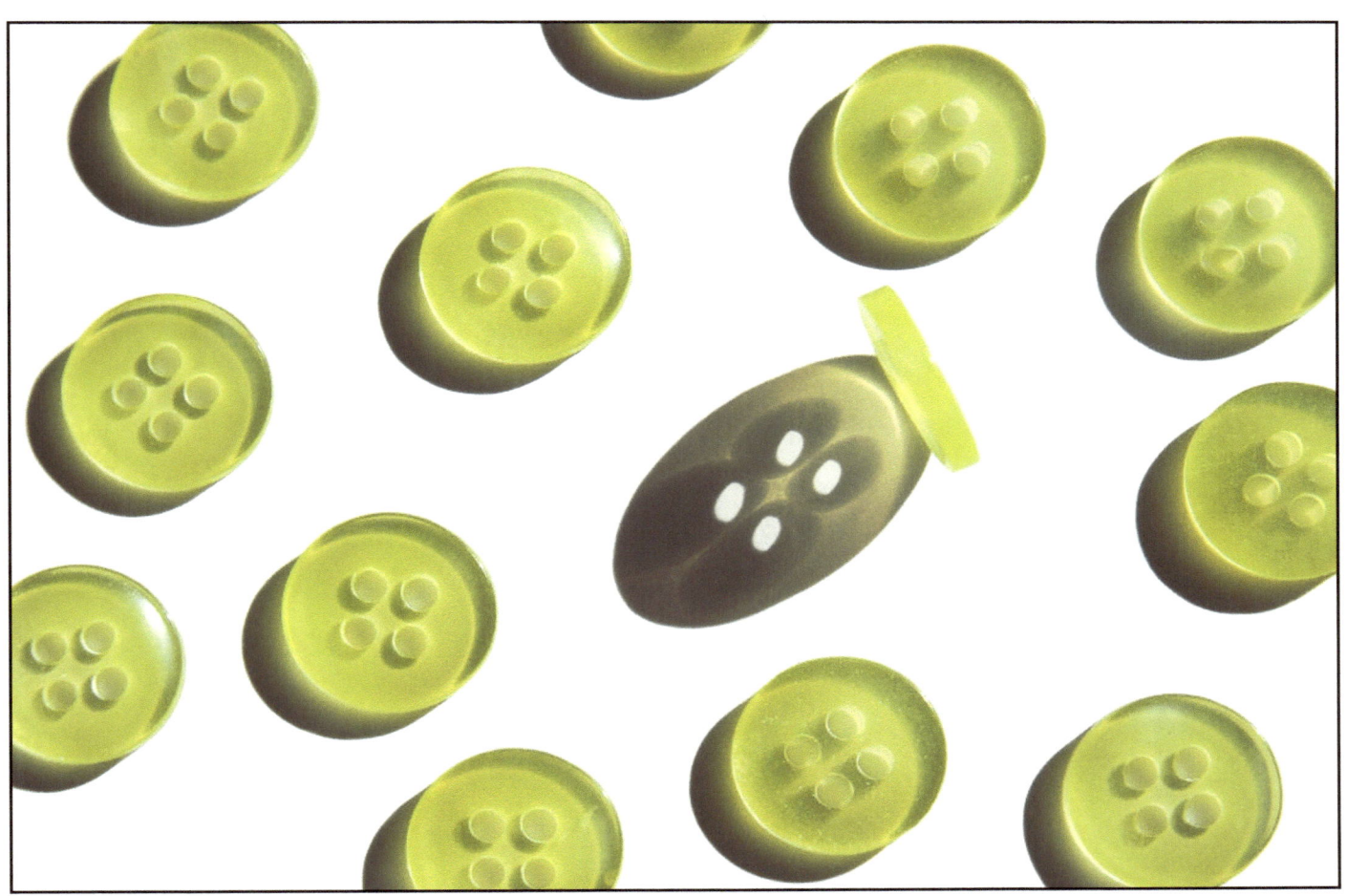

Button Up

In a button-down world, the one that's buttoned-up makes an impression.

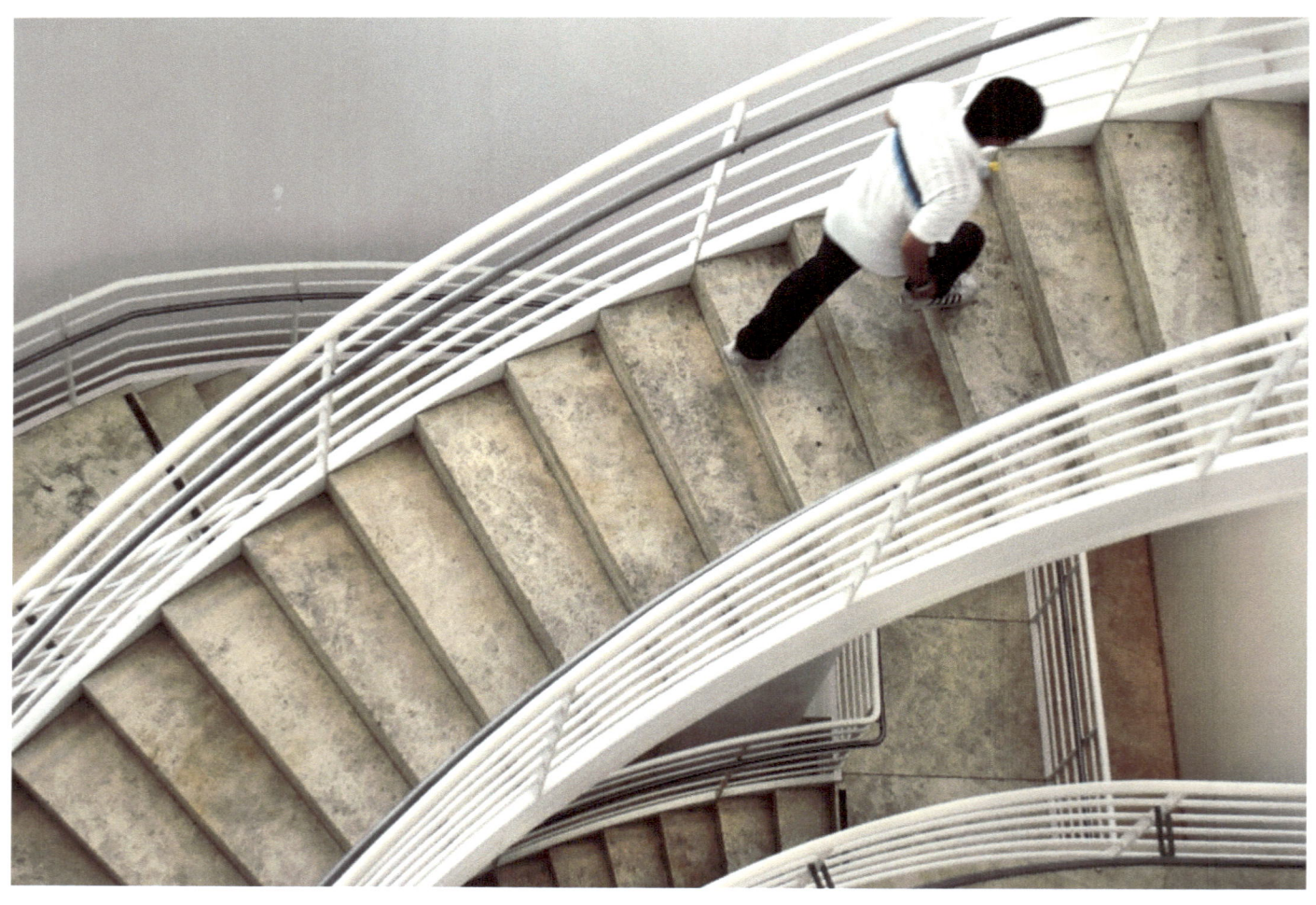

One Direction

While there were many choices, there was really only one direction.

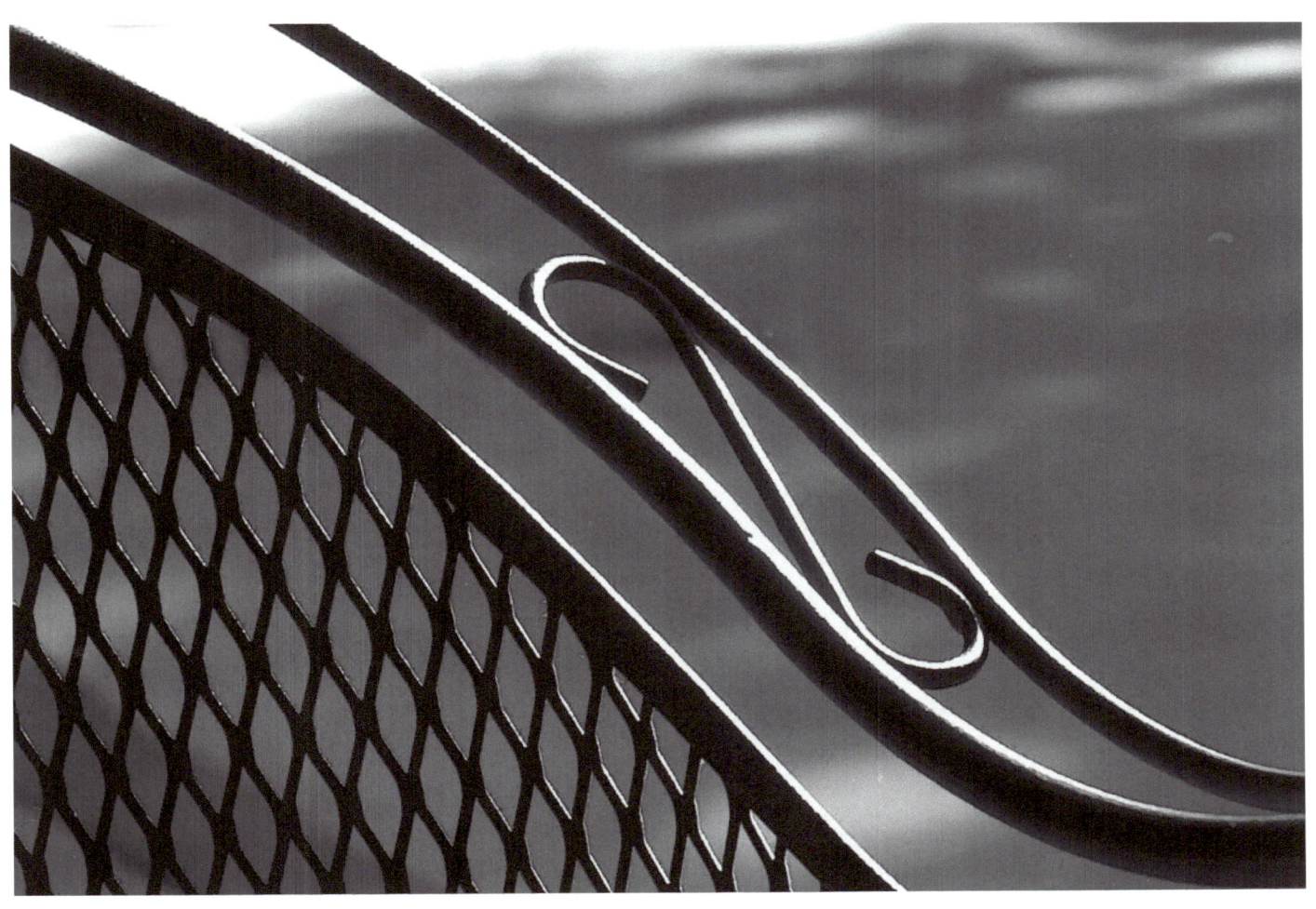

Geometry Choreography

Geometry comes to life in a graceful dance of lines and light.

Light Lunch

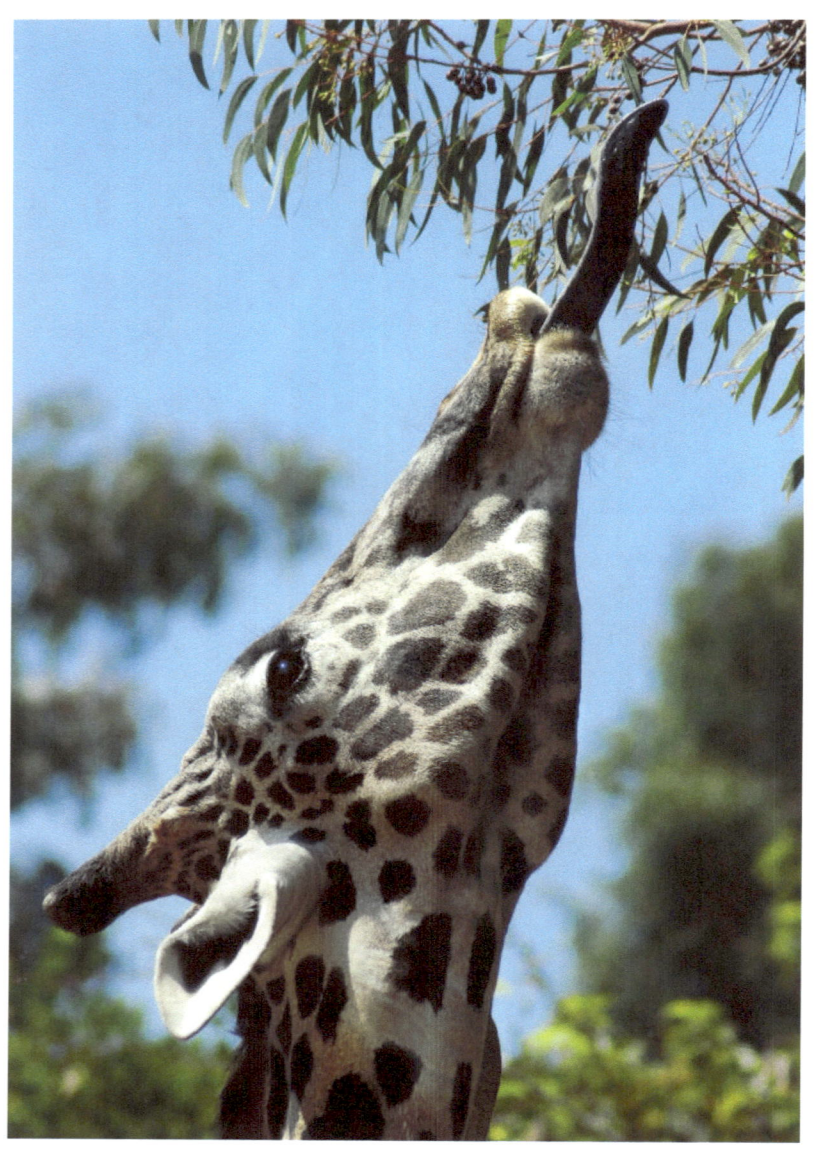

Salads usually appear at the top of the menu. Ask any giraffe.

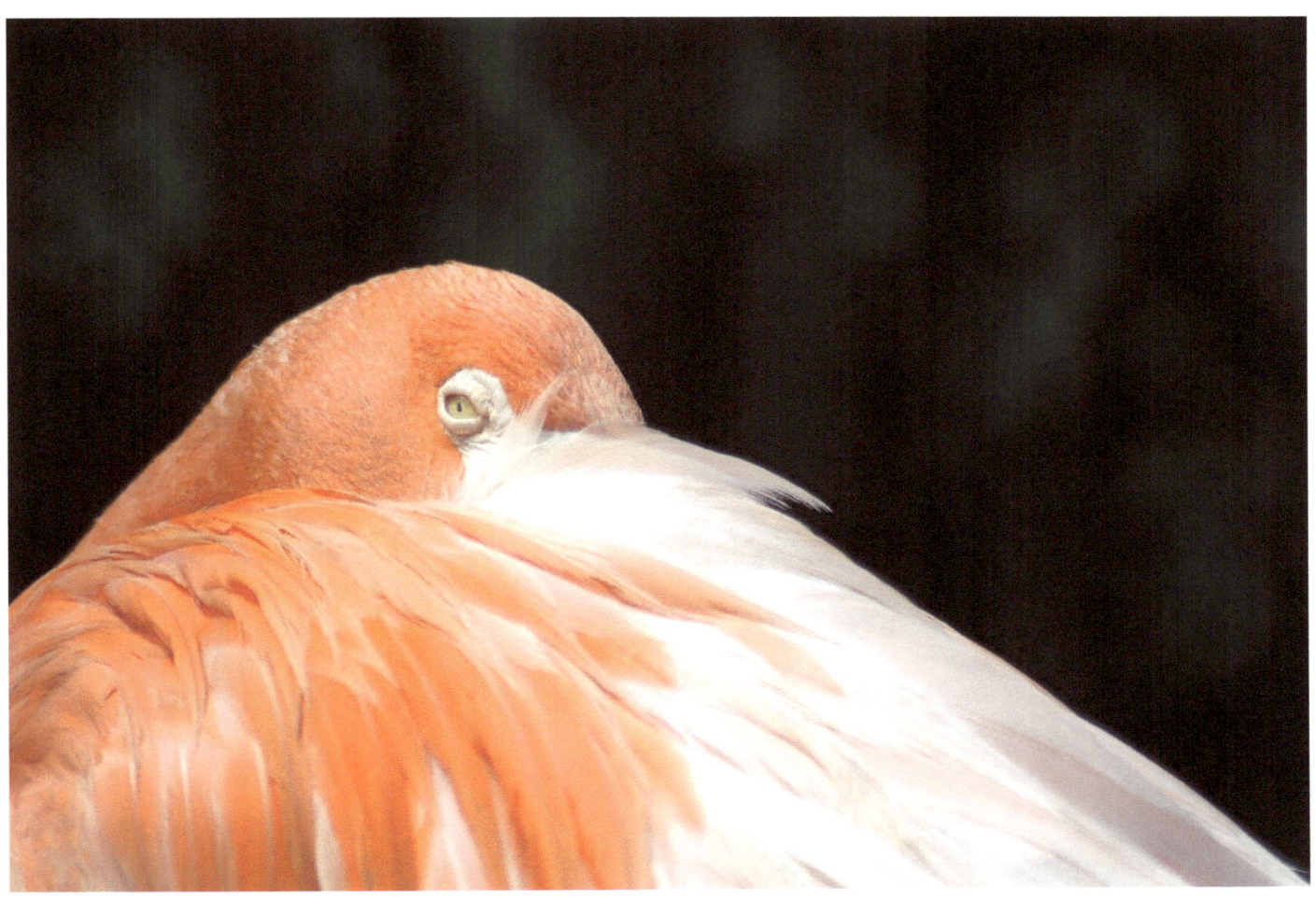

The Secret Flamingo

The flamingo guards its secrets behind a feathery cloak.

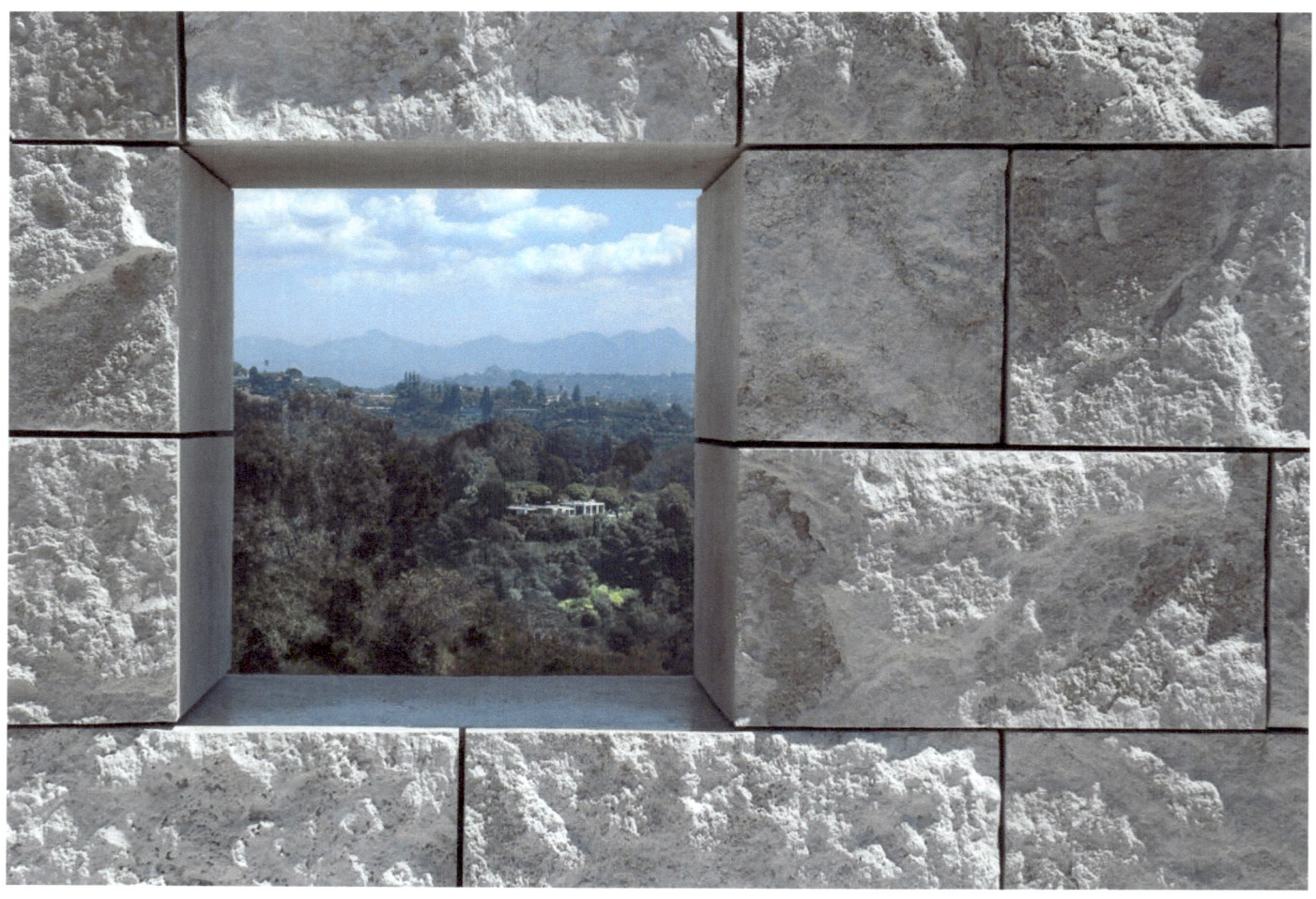

Breakthrough

The grass may be greener on the other side but there's a world of detail to explore right over here.

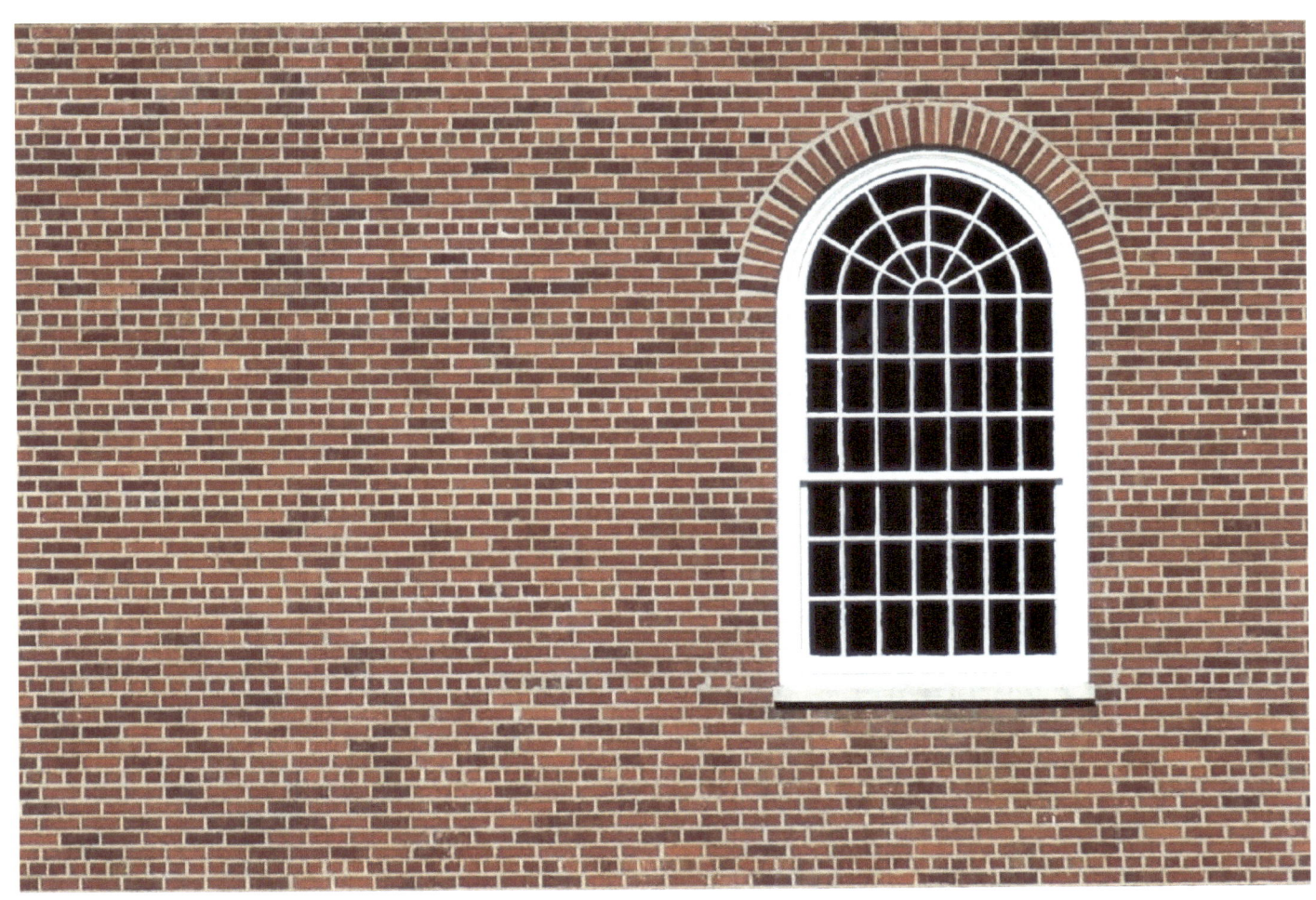

Wall And Window

It's not about the wall, it's about the hole in the wall.

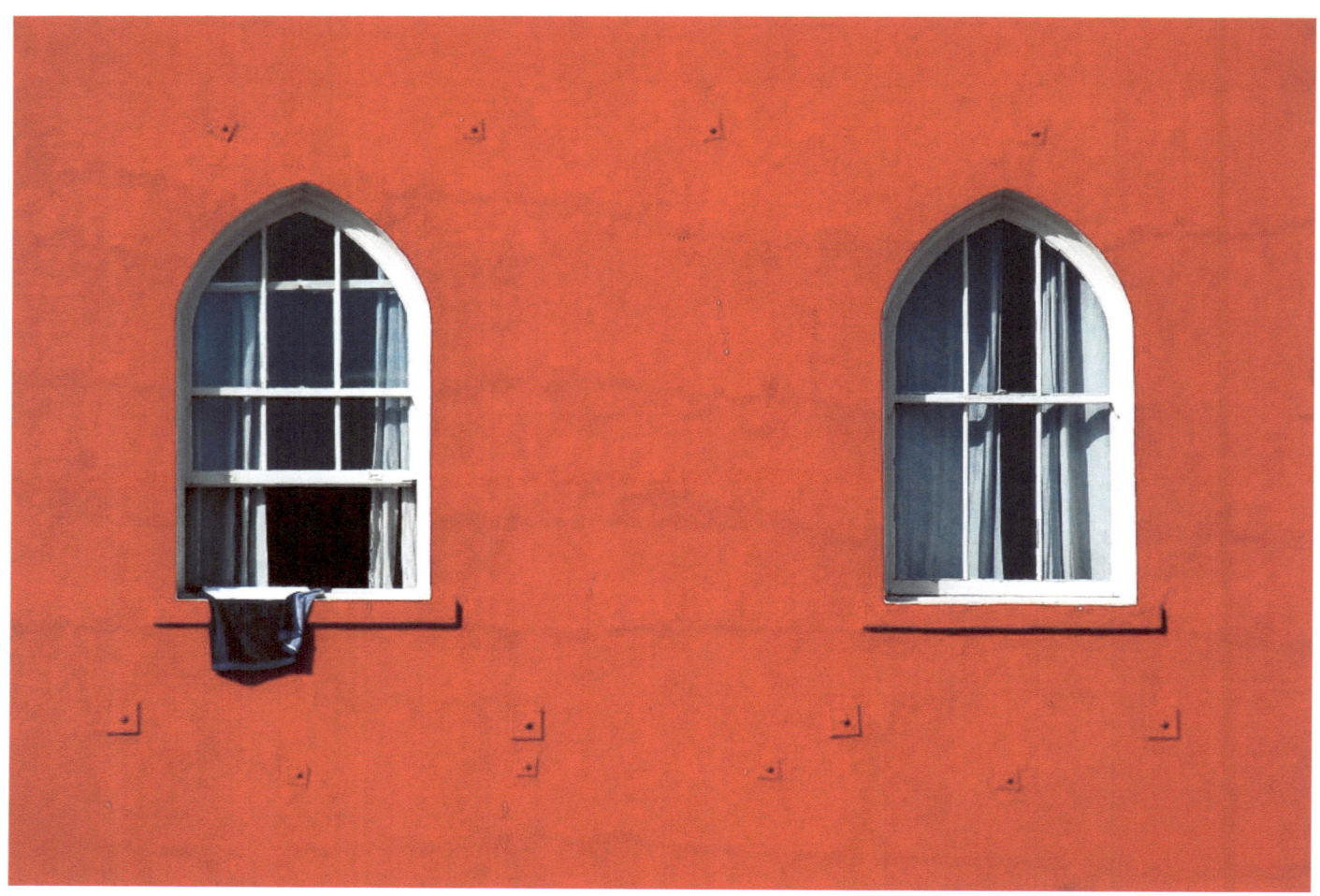

Two Windows

Two windows, each with its own personality, each with its own story to tell.

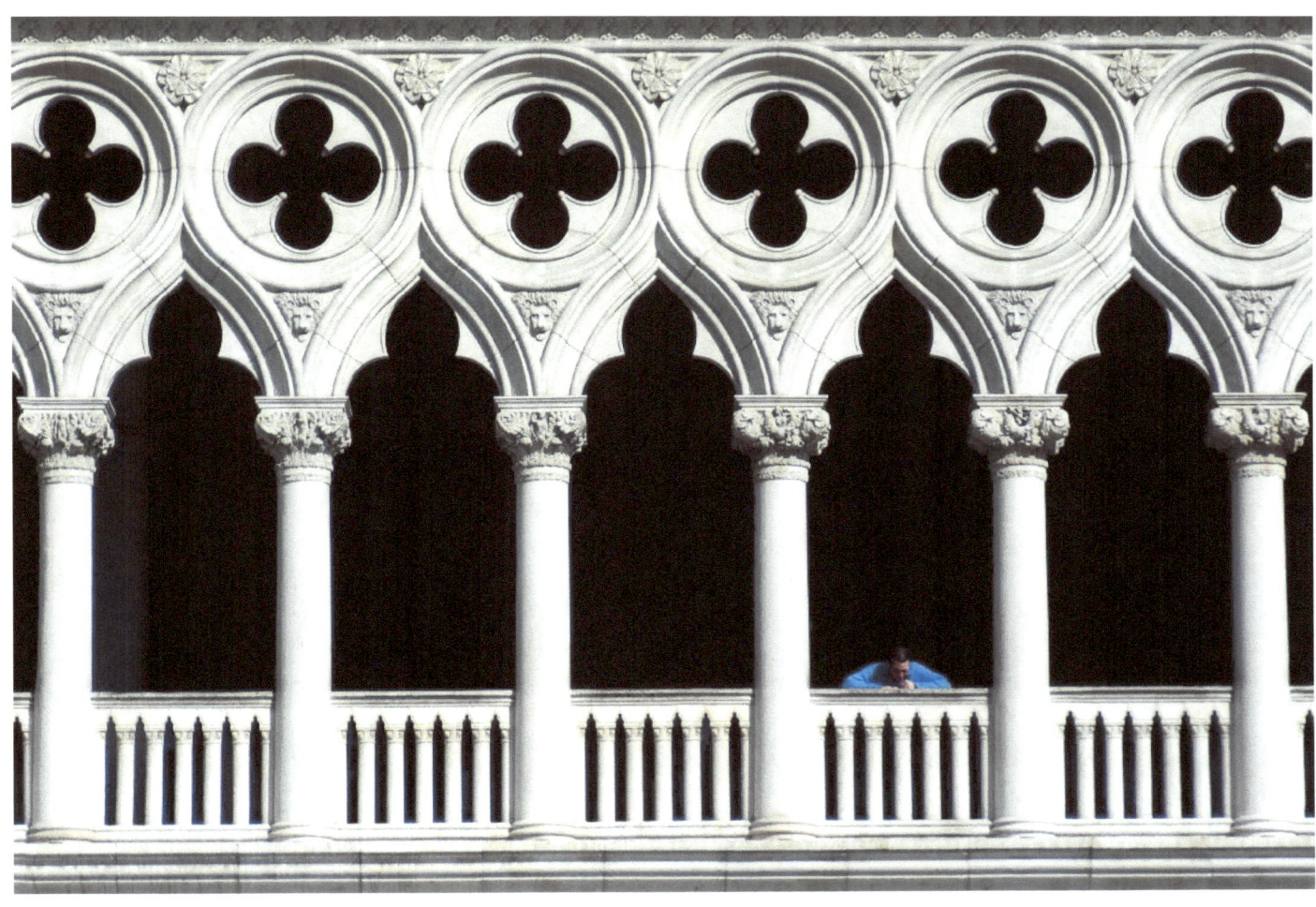

Grand Design

Whether he knew it or not, he was part of a grand design.

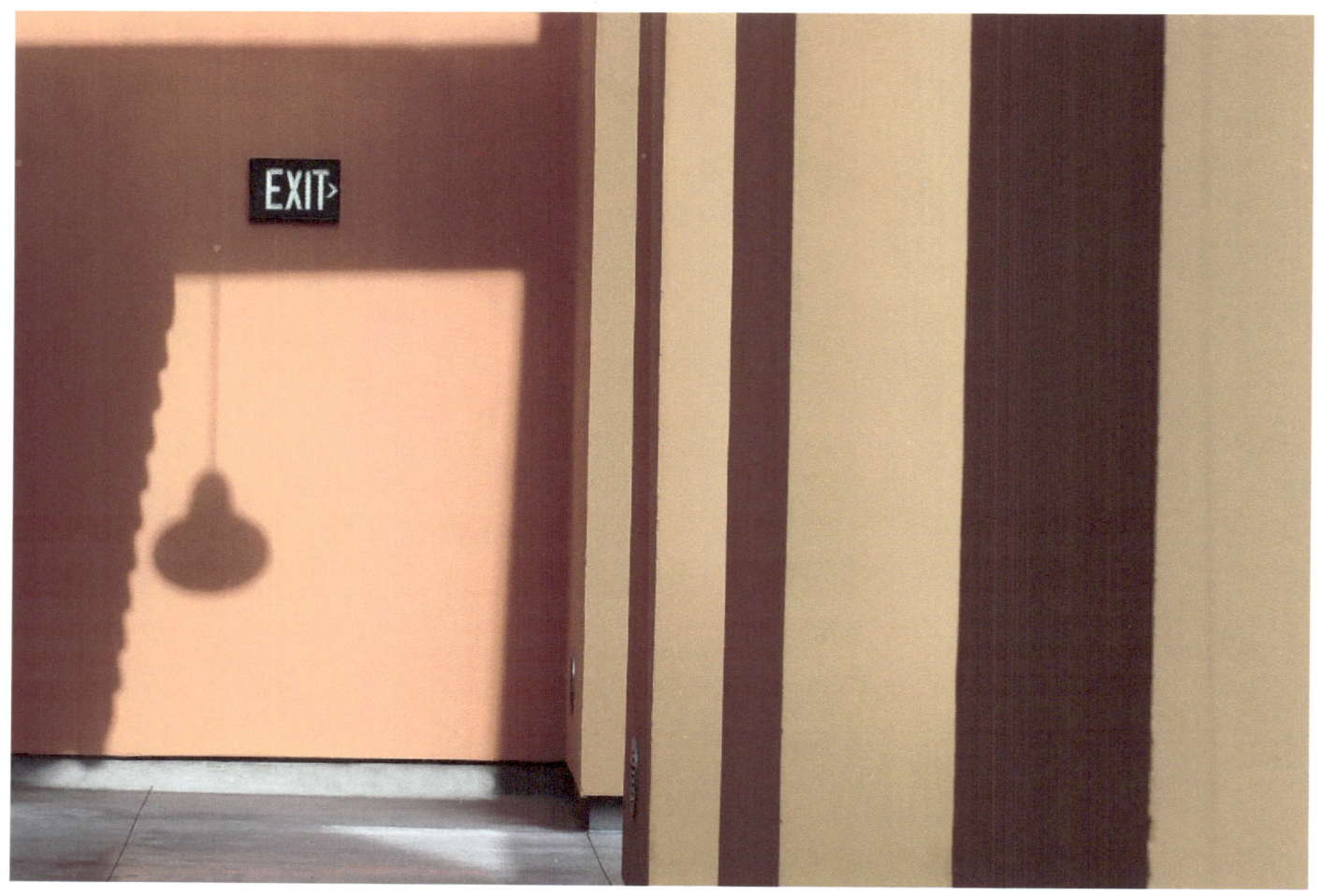

Hall Light

To exit, just go to the light at the end of the hall and turn right.

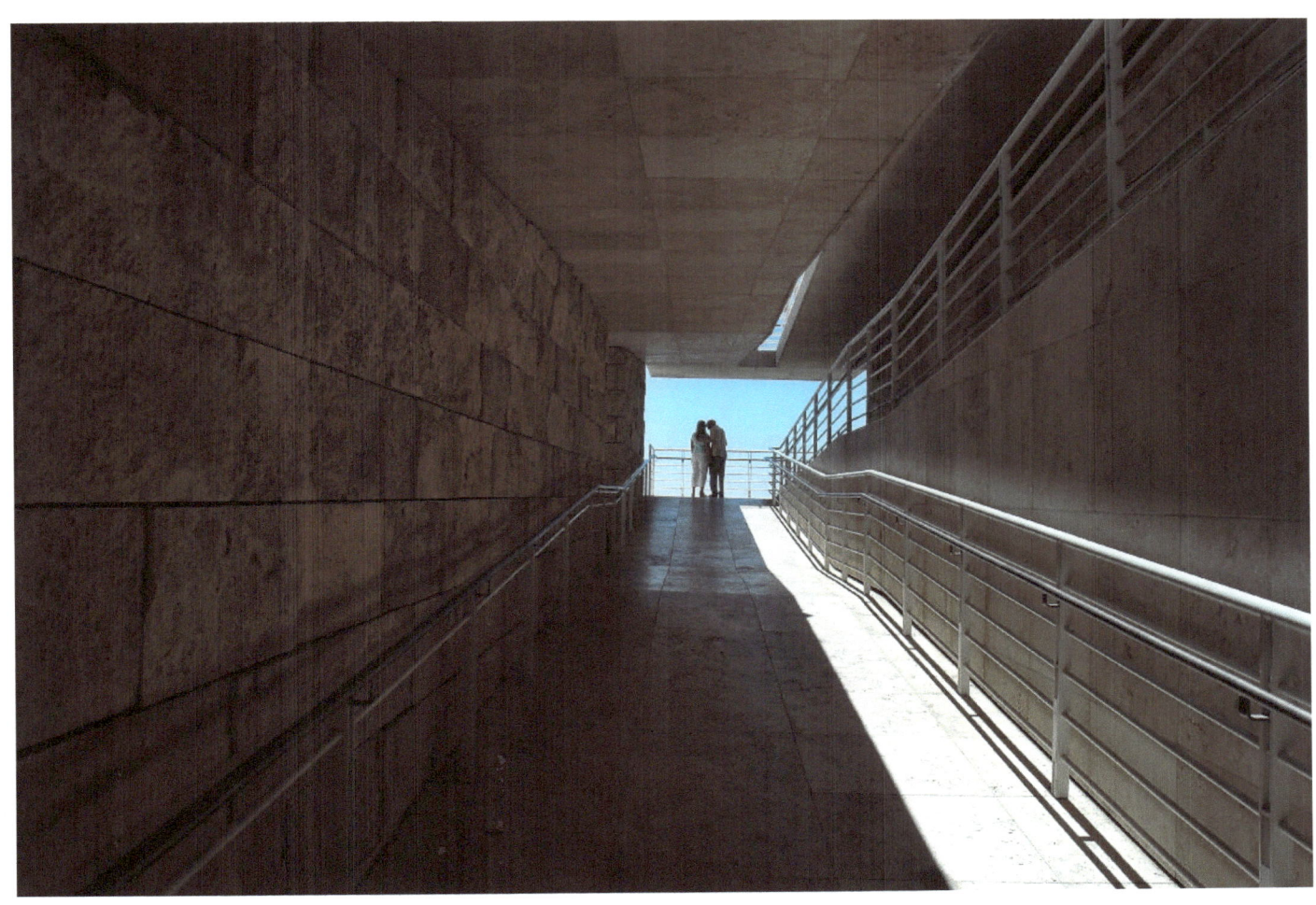

Along The Way

They stopped along the way to take time for themselves.

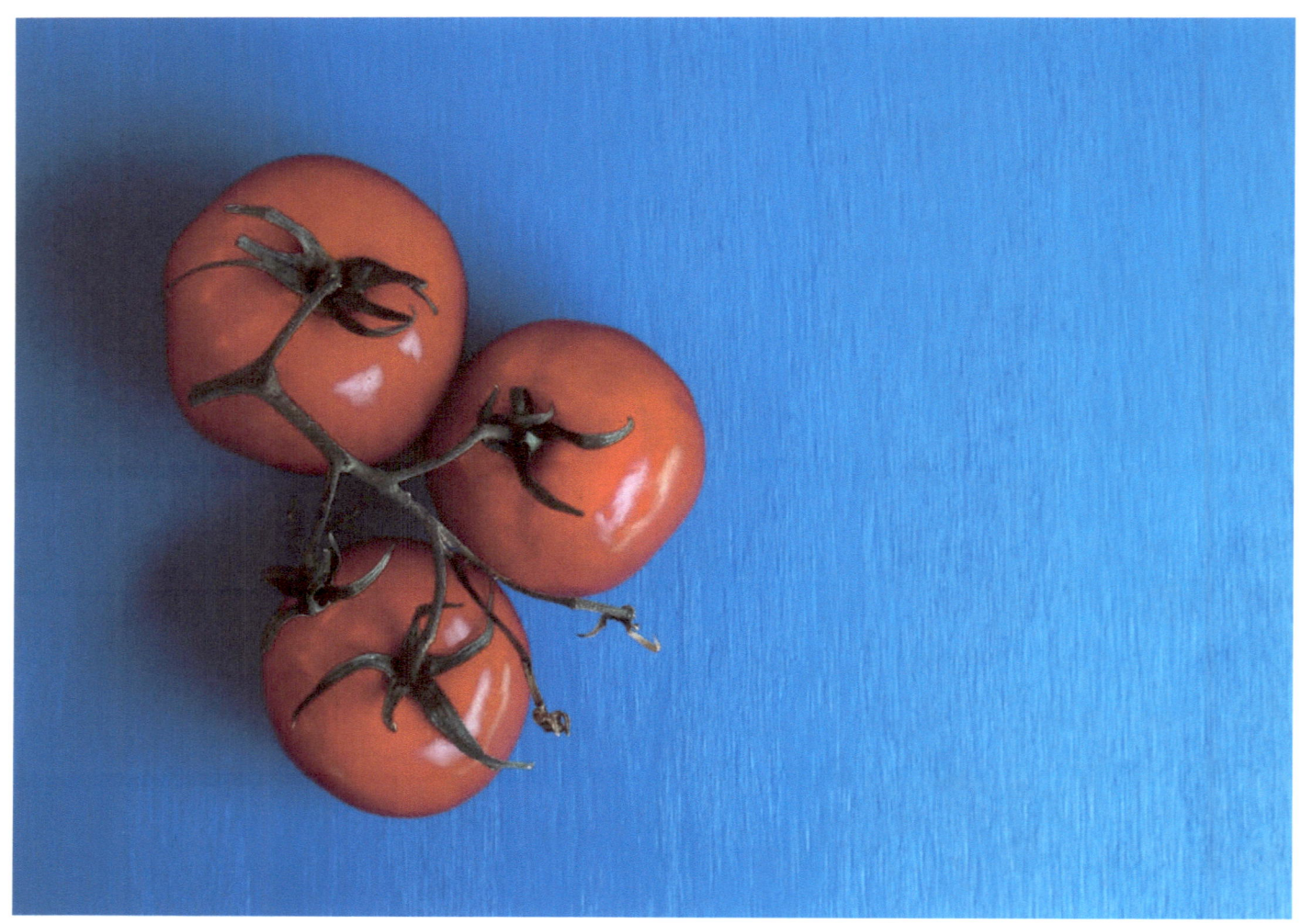

Threematoes

Threematoes are better than twomatoes. In this case, anyway.

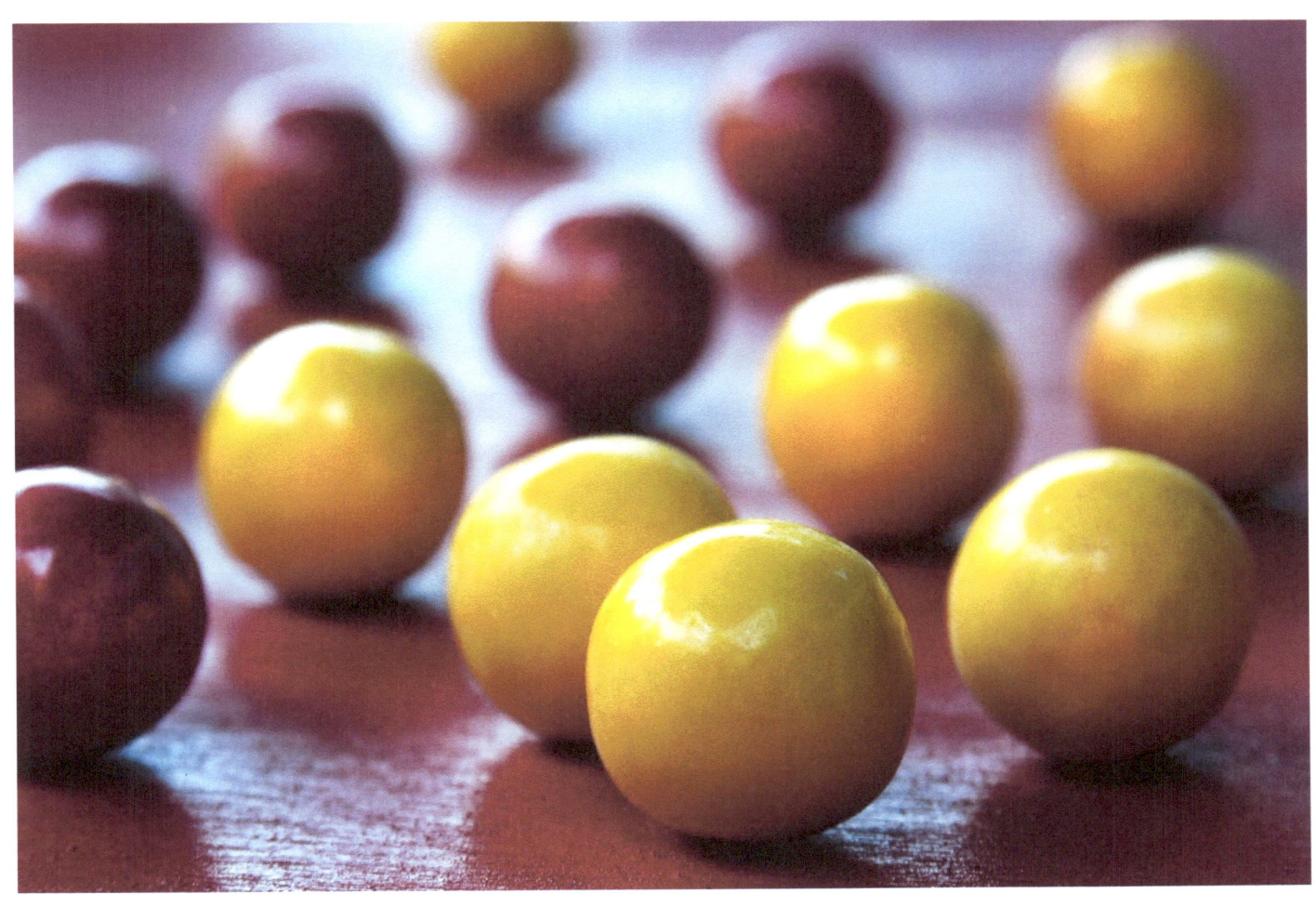

Gumball Gathering

Once they realized their similarities were greater than their differences, they all got along just fine.

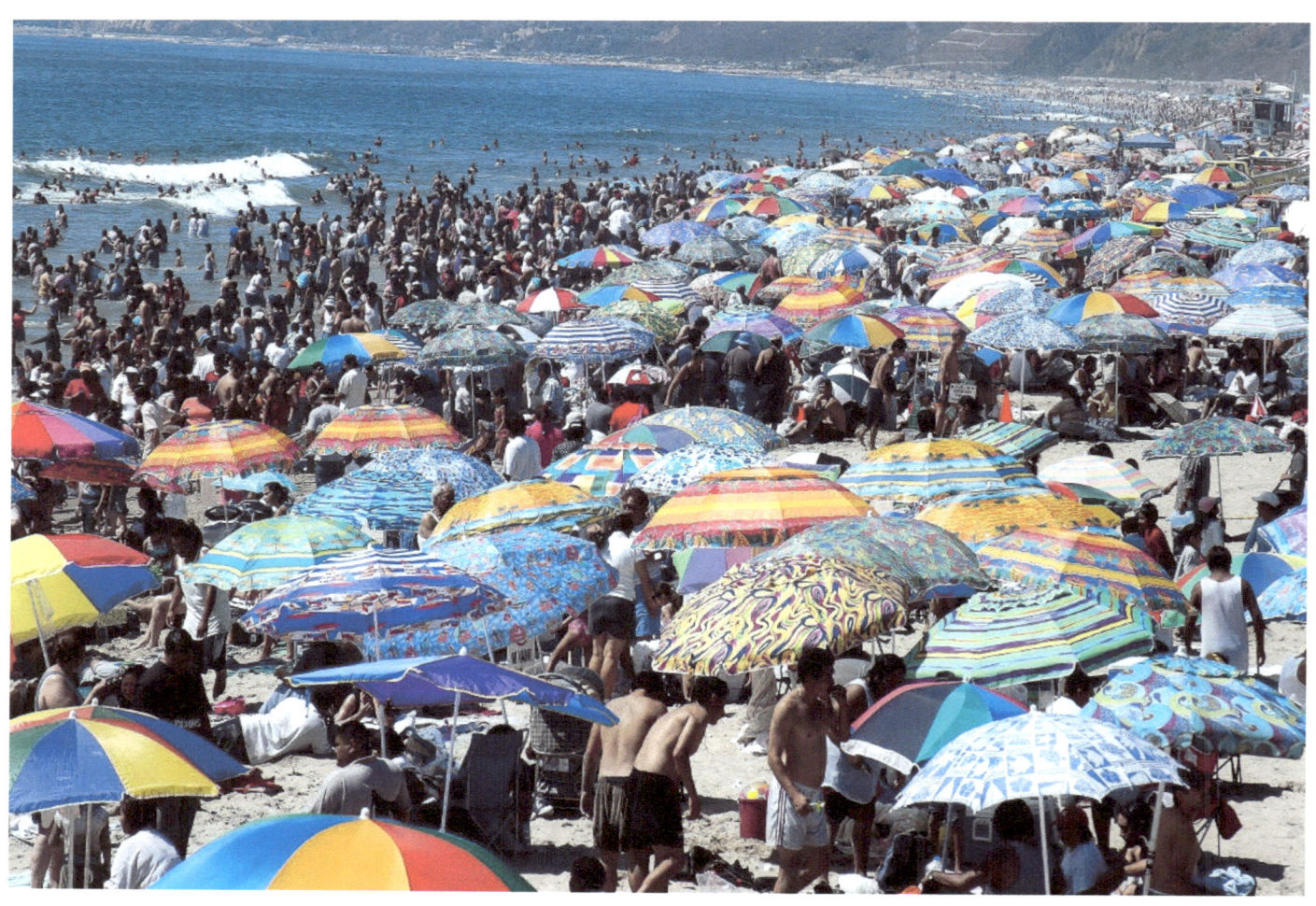

It's A Beach

They came to enjoy the sun and the surf. And so did everybody else.

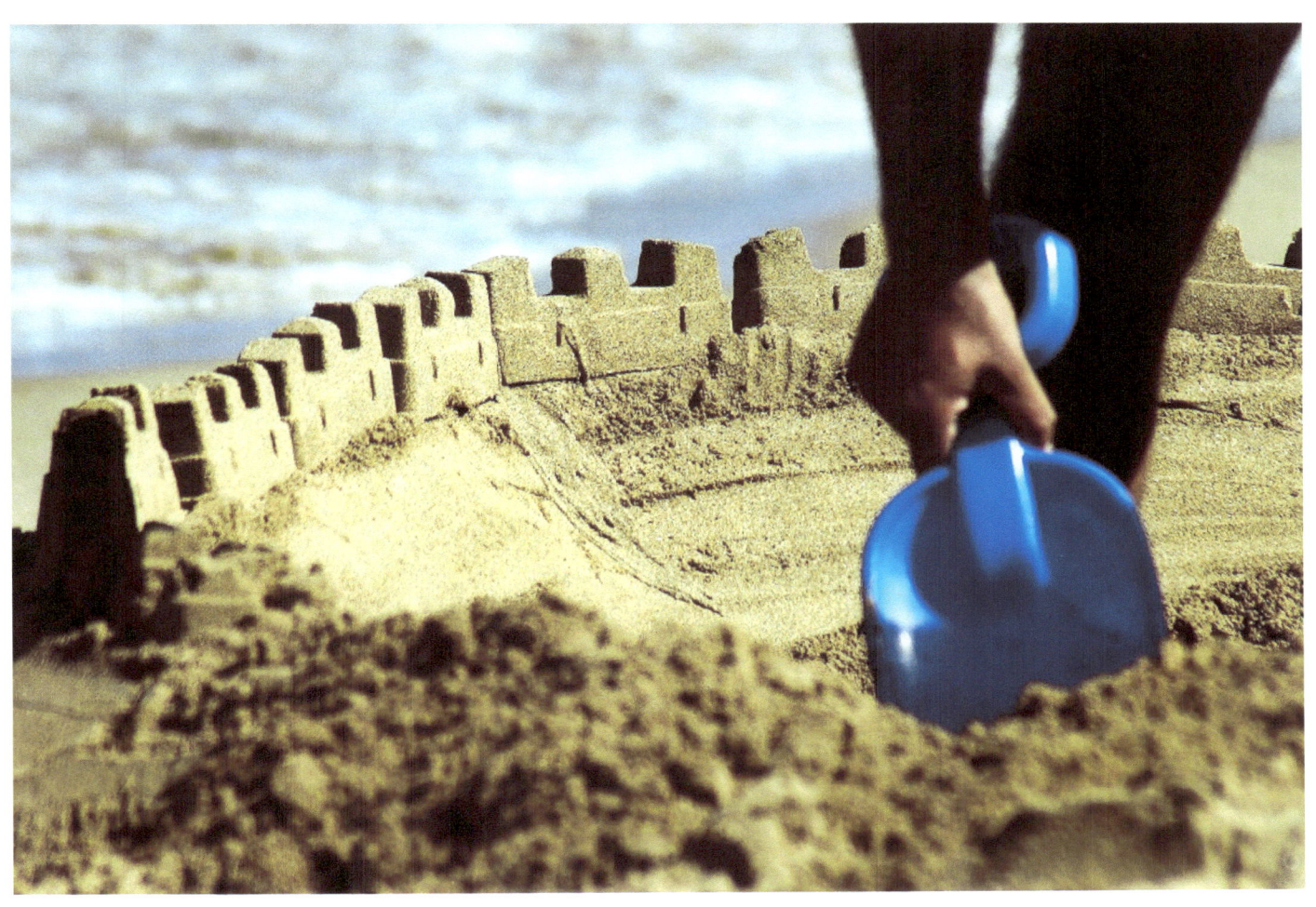

Castle By The Sea

It wasn't fancy but it was built with pride.

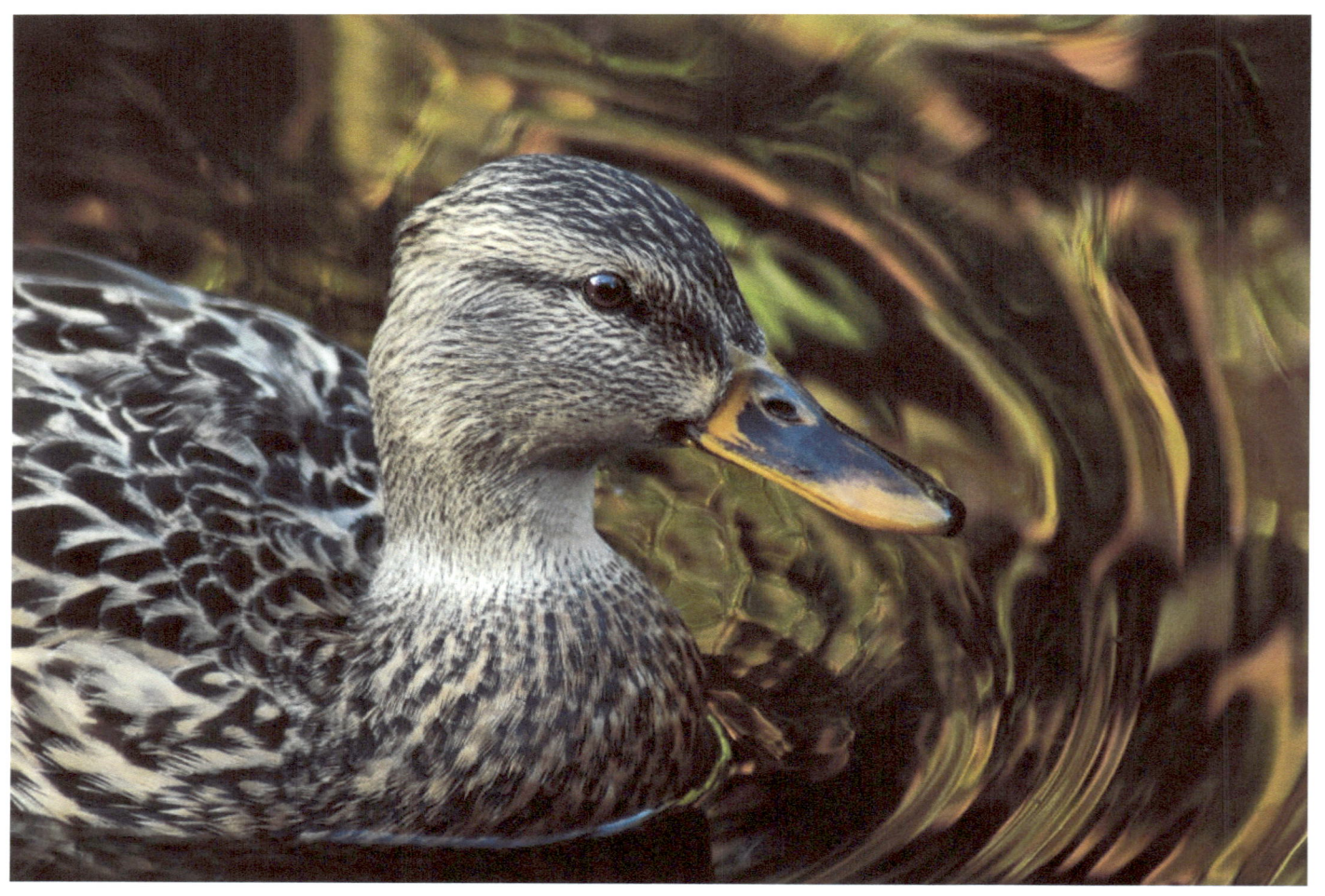

Smooth Ride

A fluid glide through molten colors.

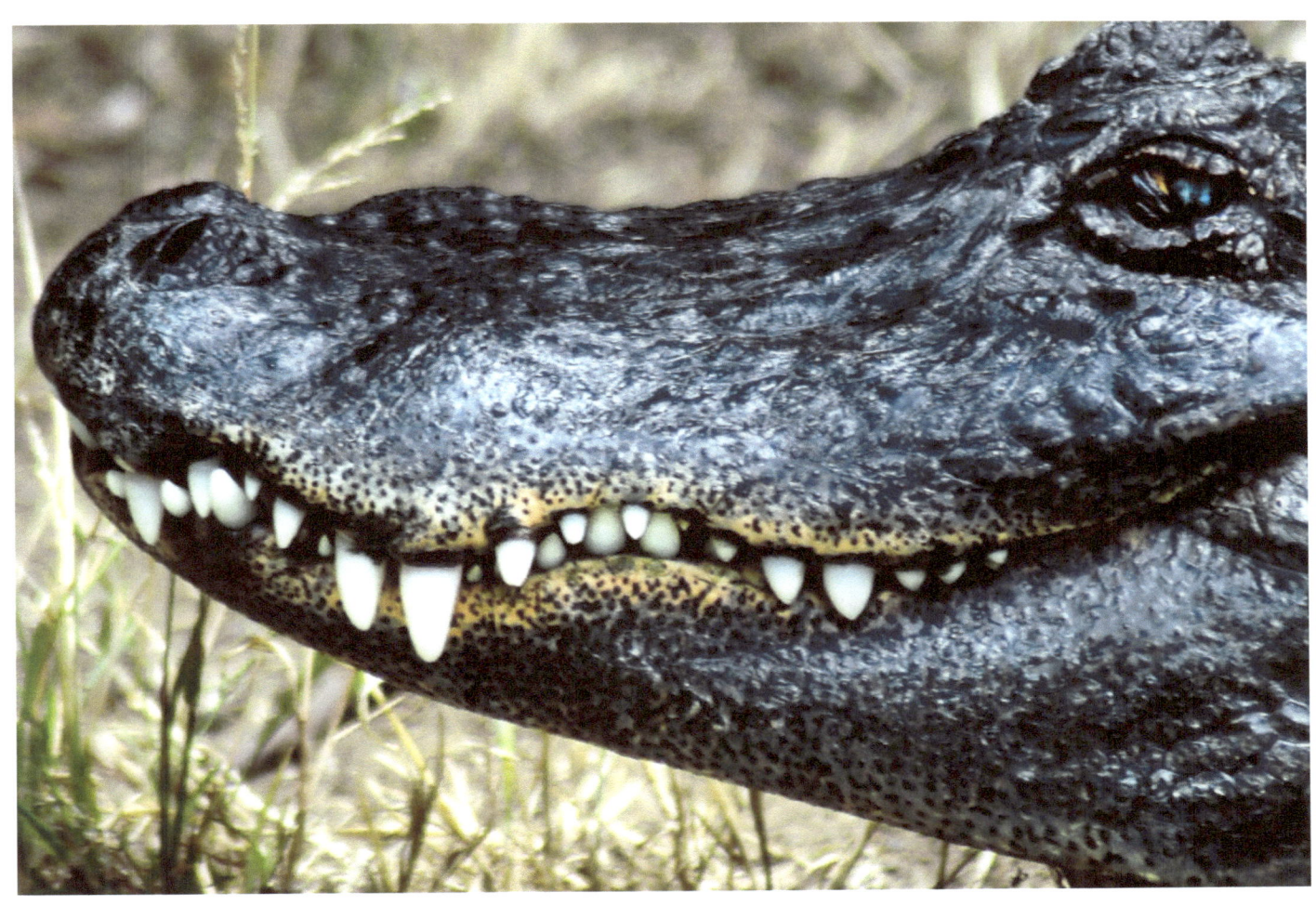

Crooked Smile

He seemed like a nice enough guy. I mean, he was always smiling ....

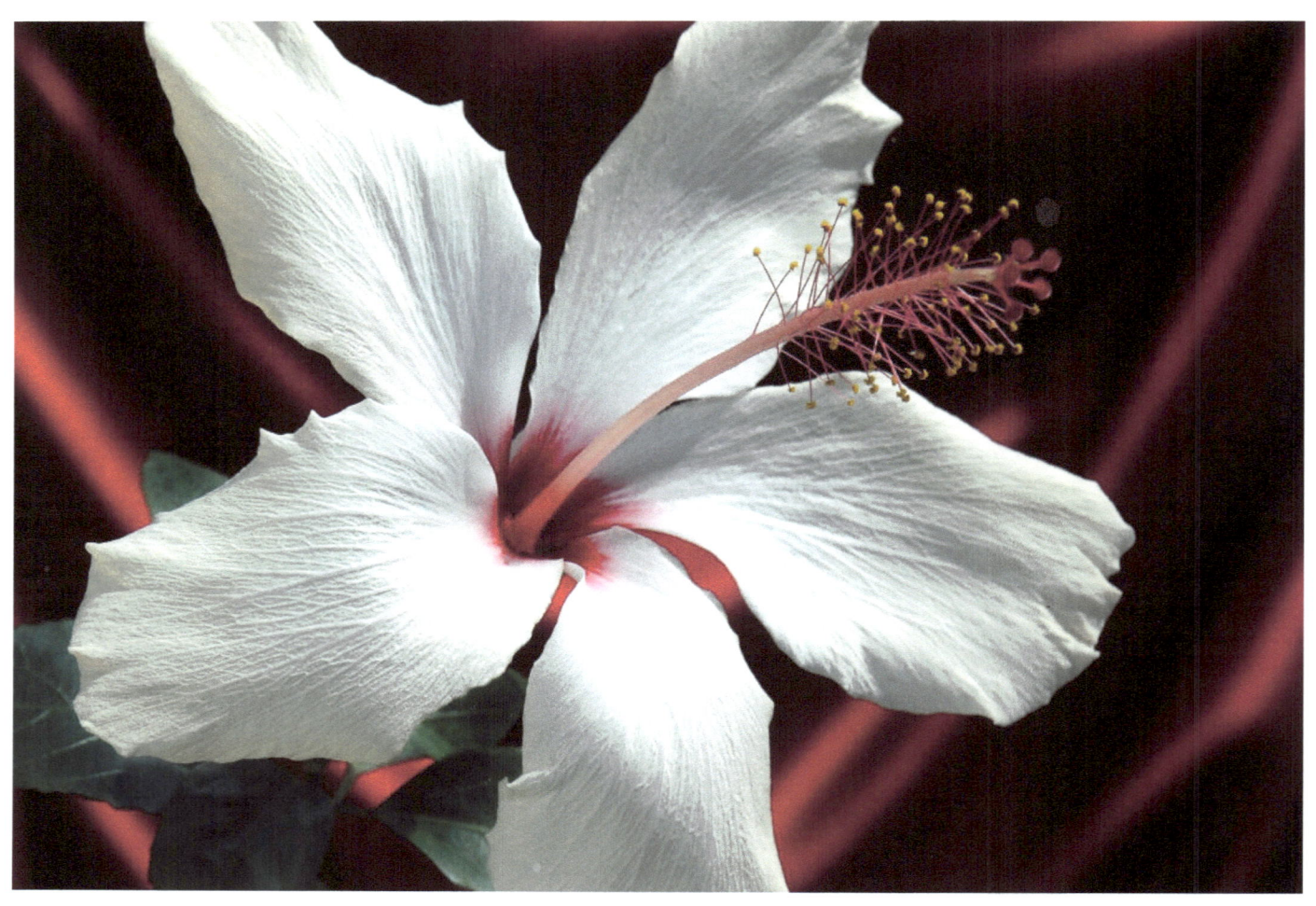

Draped With Detail

Flowing design, draped with detail and color.

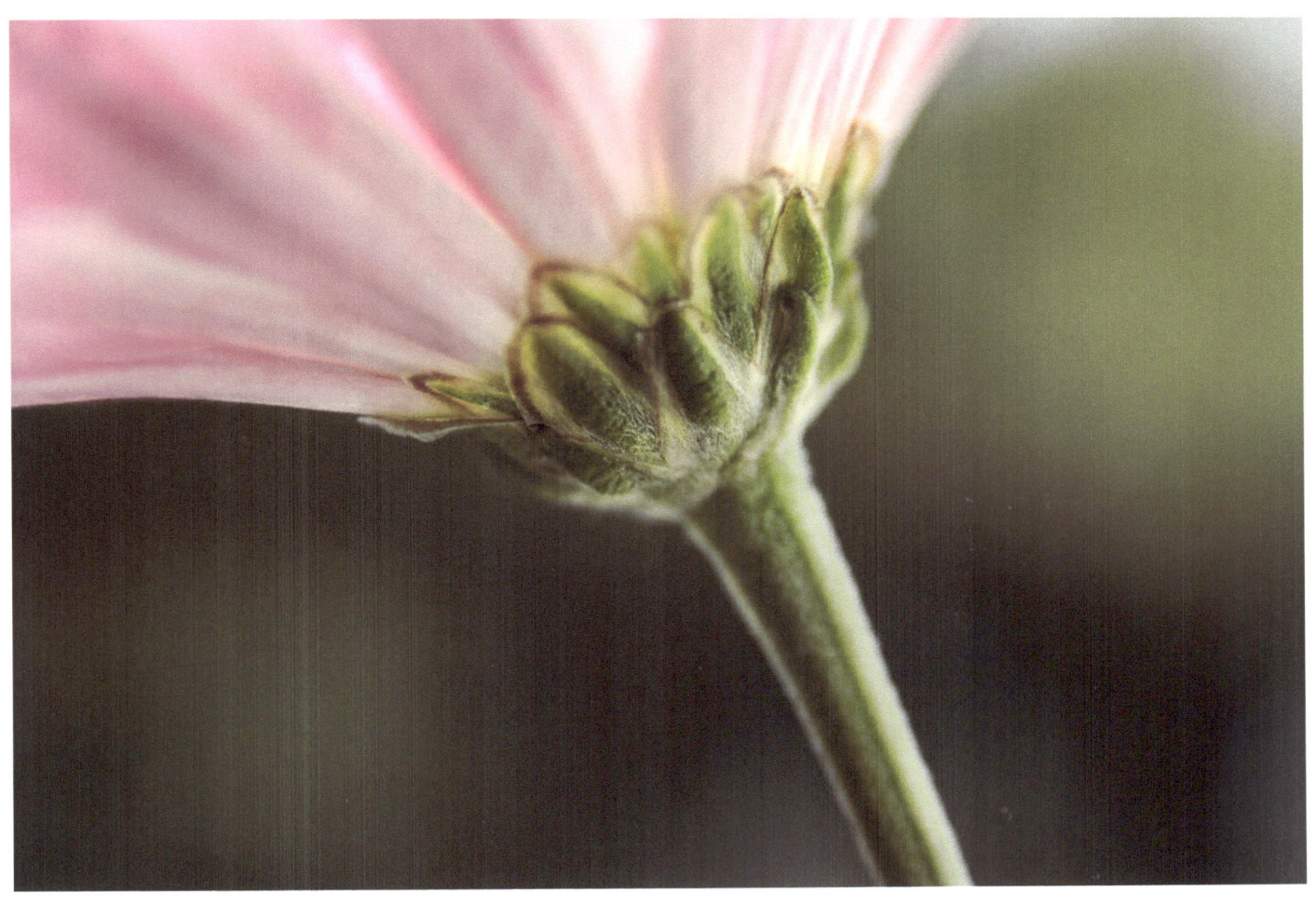

Under The Canopy

Under a colorful canopy, the stem meets the petals and the details work themselves out.

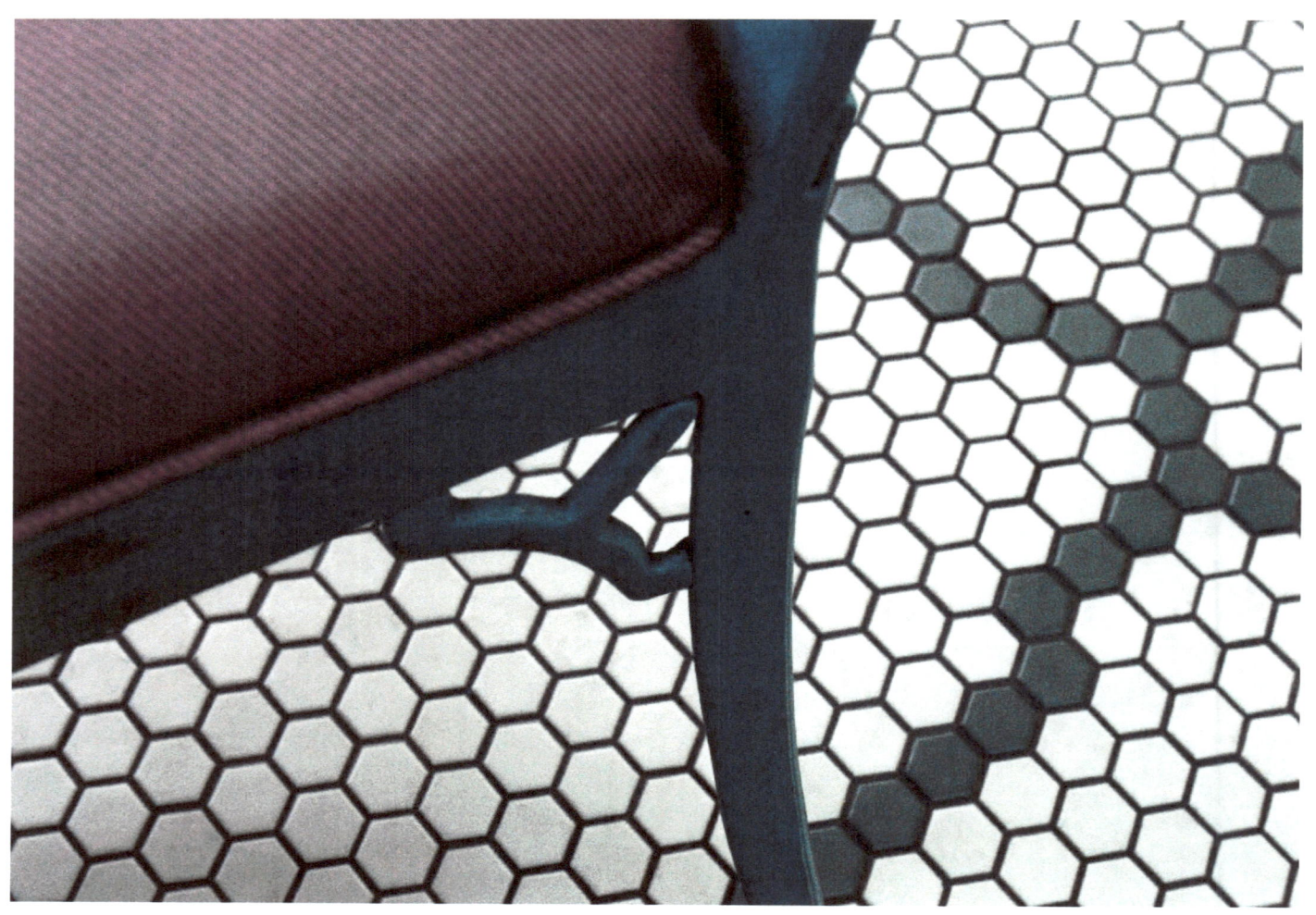

On The Floor

A busy world of pattern and color down there under the chair.

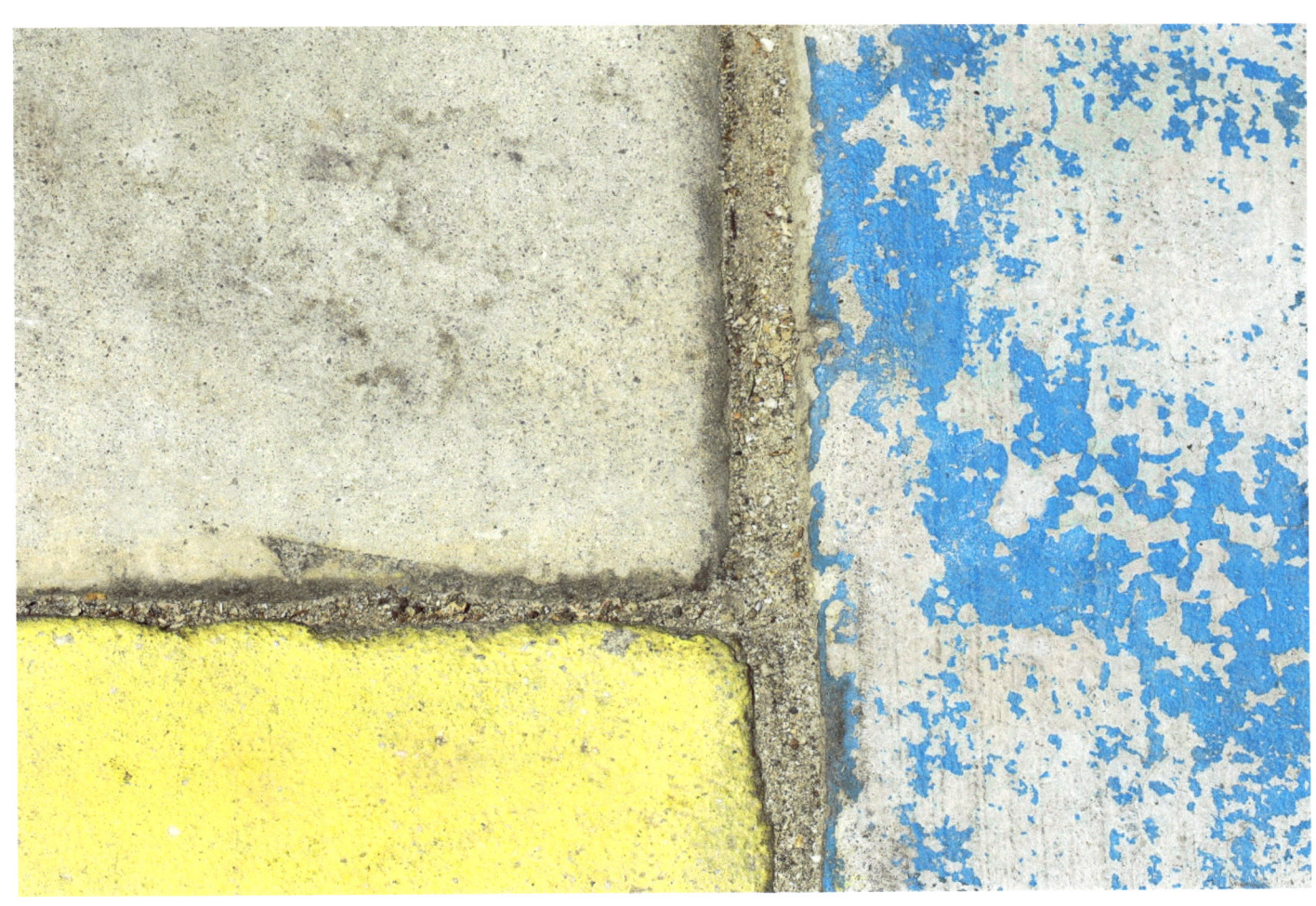

The Next Step

With every step, the landscape changes, the pieces fit differently.

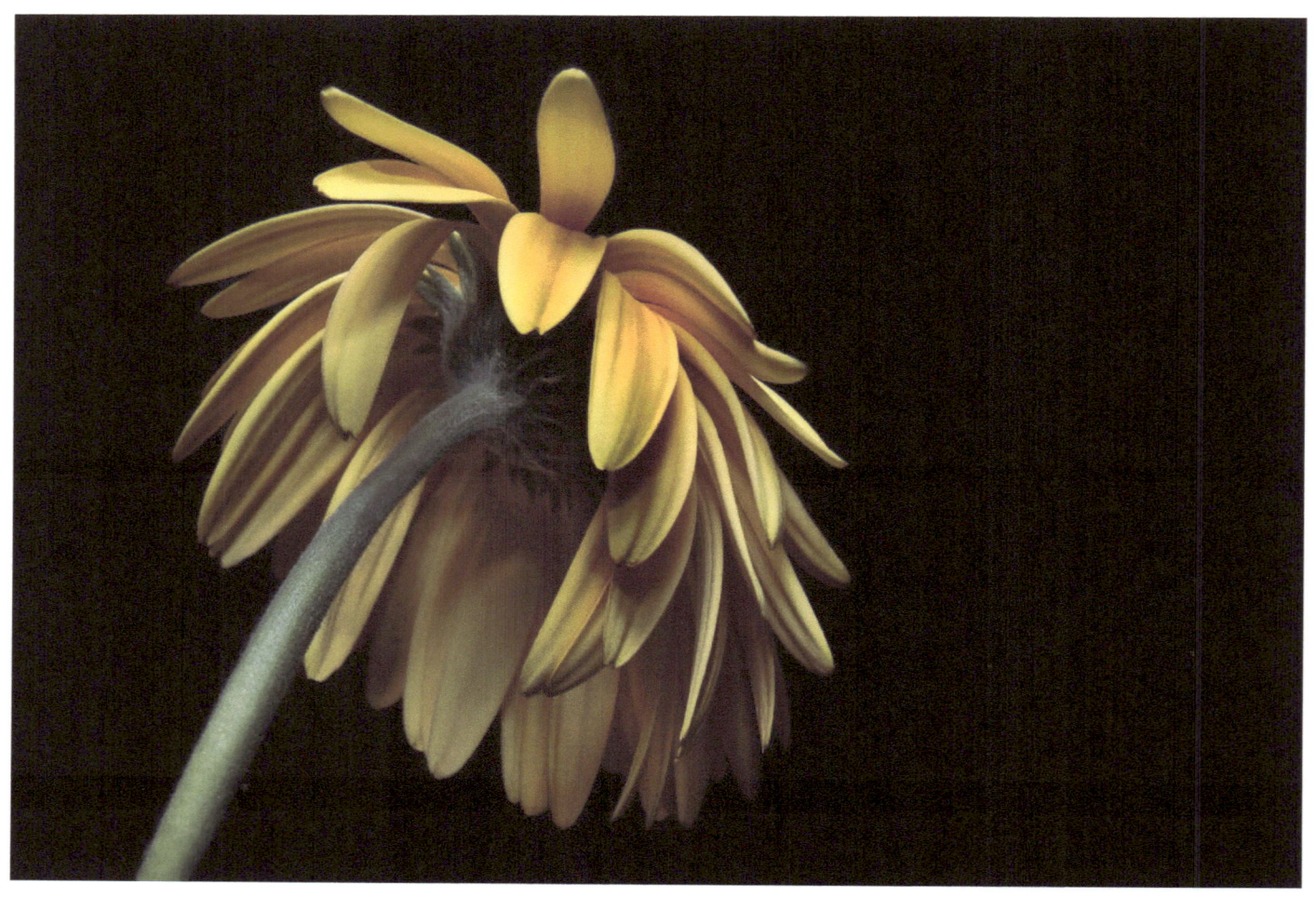

Between

A special kind of elegance happens as the flower evolves from what it was to what it will inevitably become.

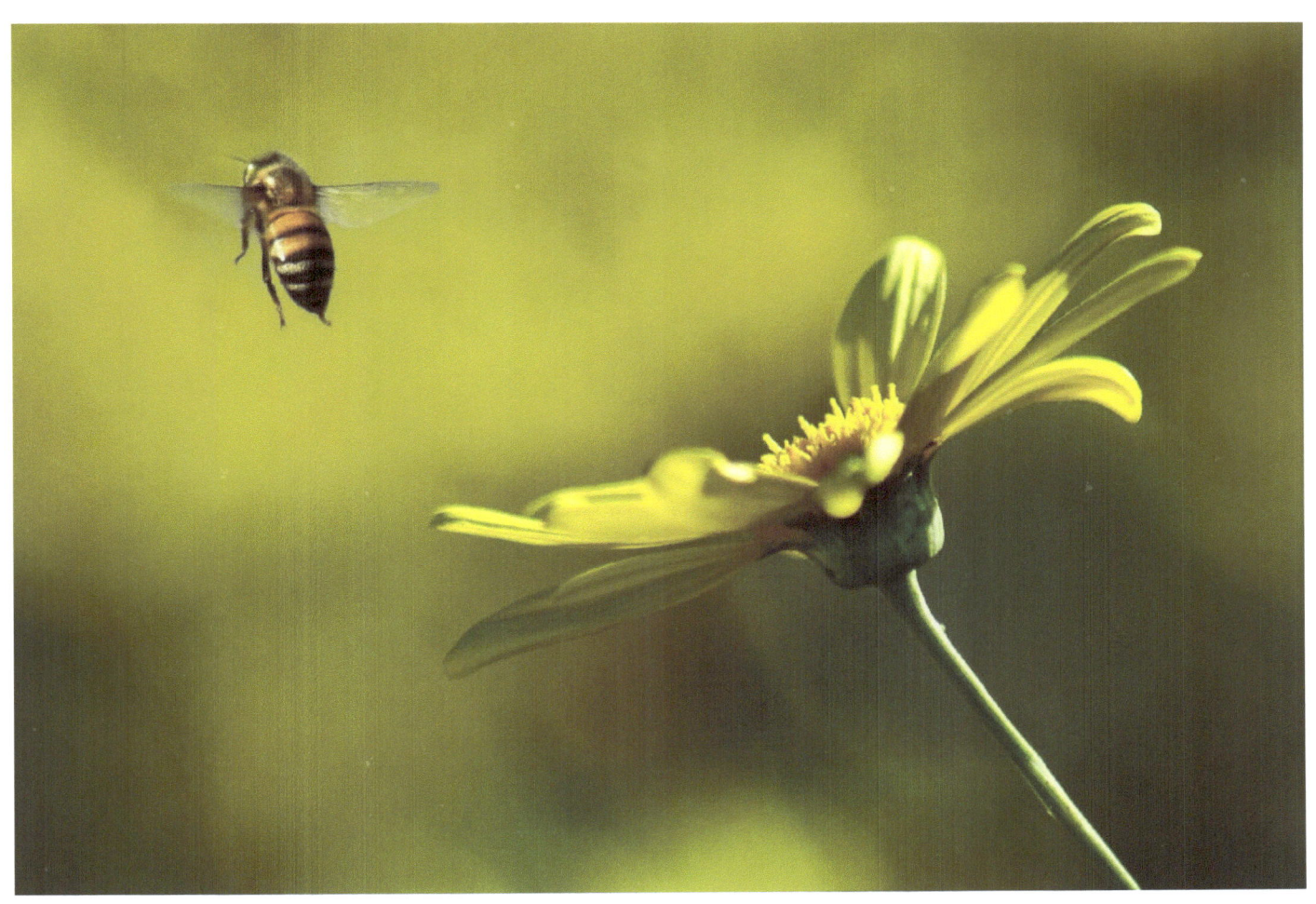

Golden Wings

Nature never stops, moving from one miracle to the next on golden wings.

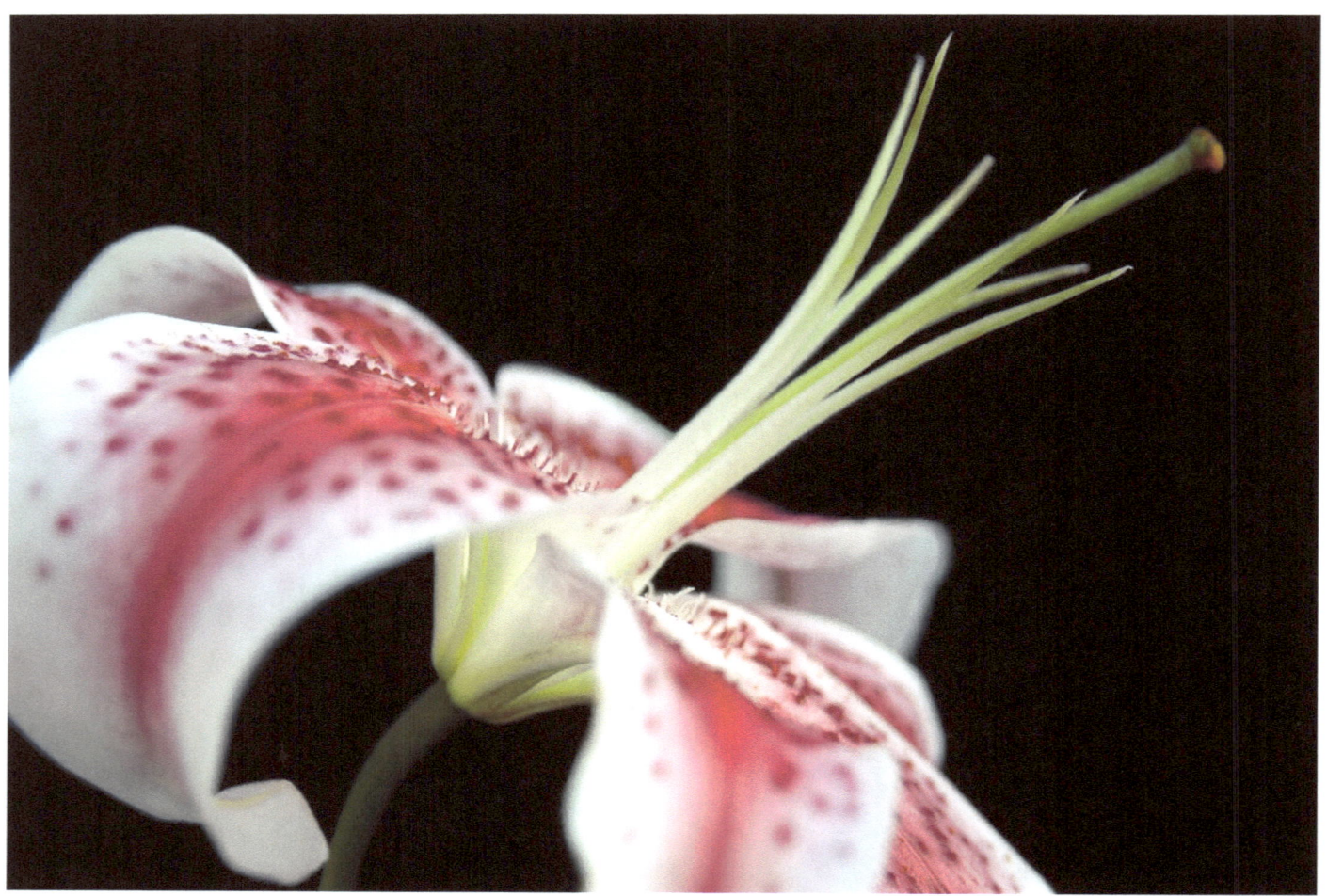

Beacon

The beacon draws attention; a signal to stop and look.

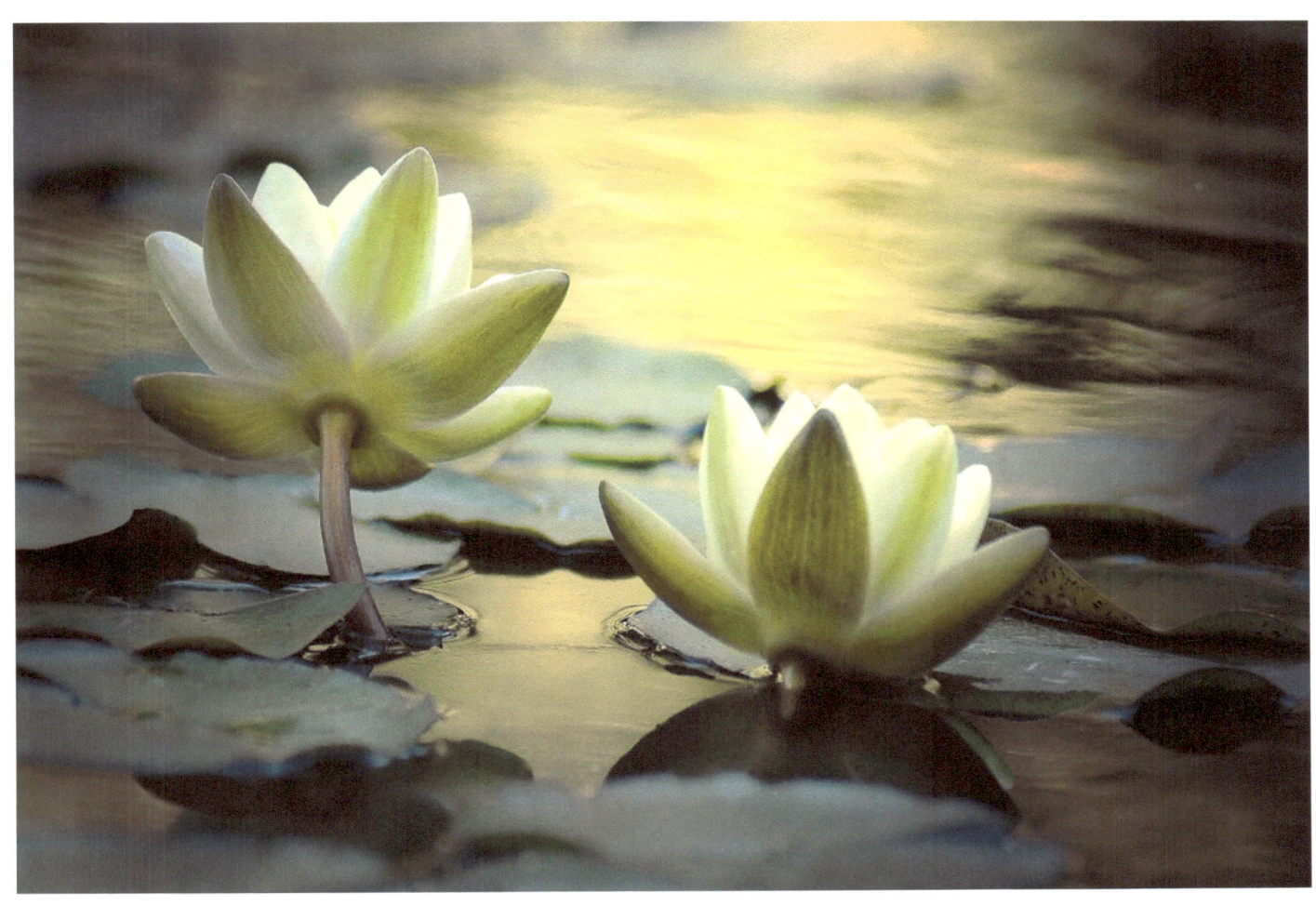

Flowers Afloat

Although they had drifted apart for a while, they came together to share the sunset.

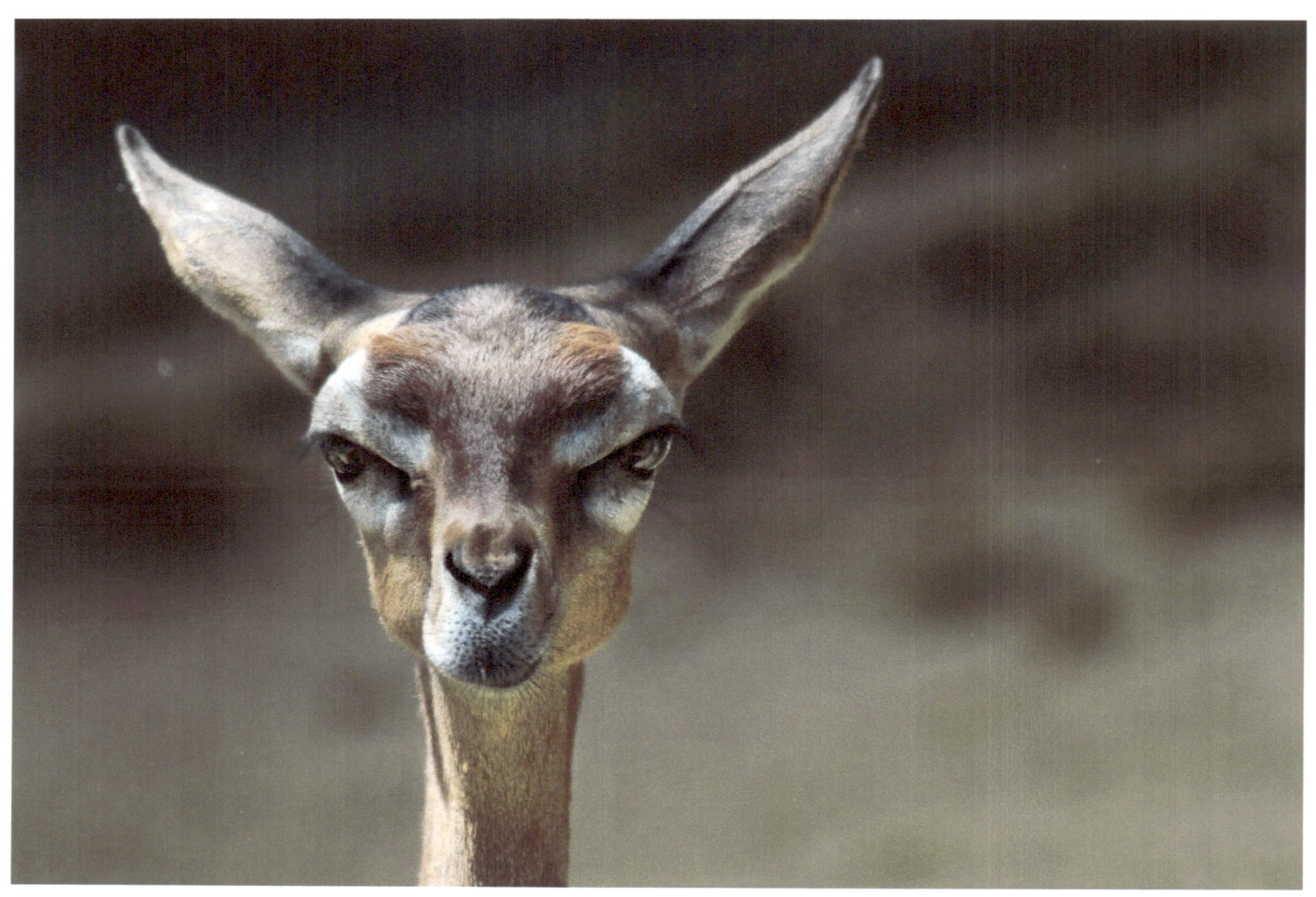

Staredown

Eventually, I blinked.

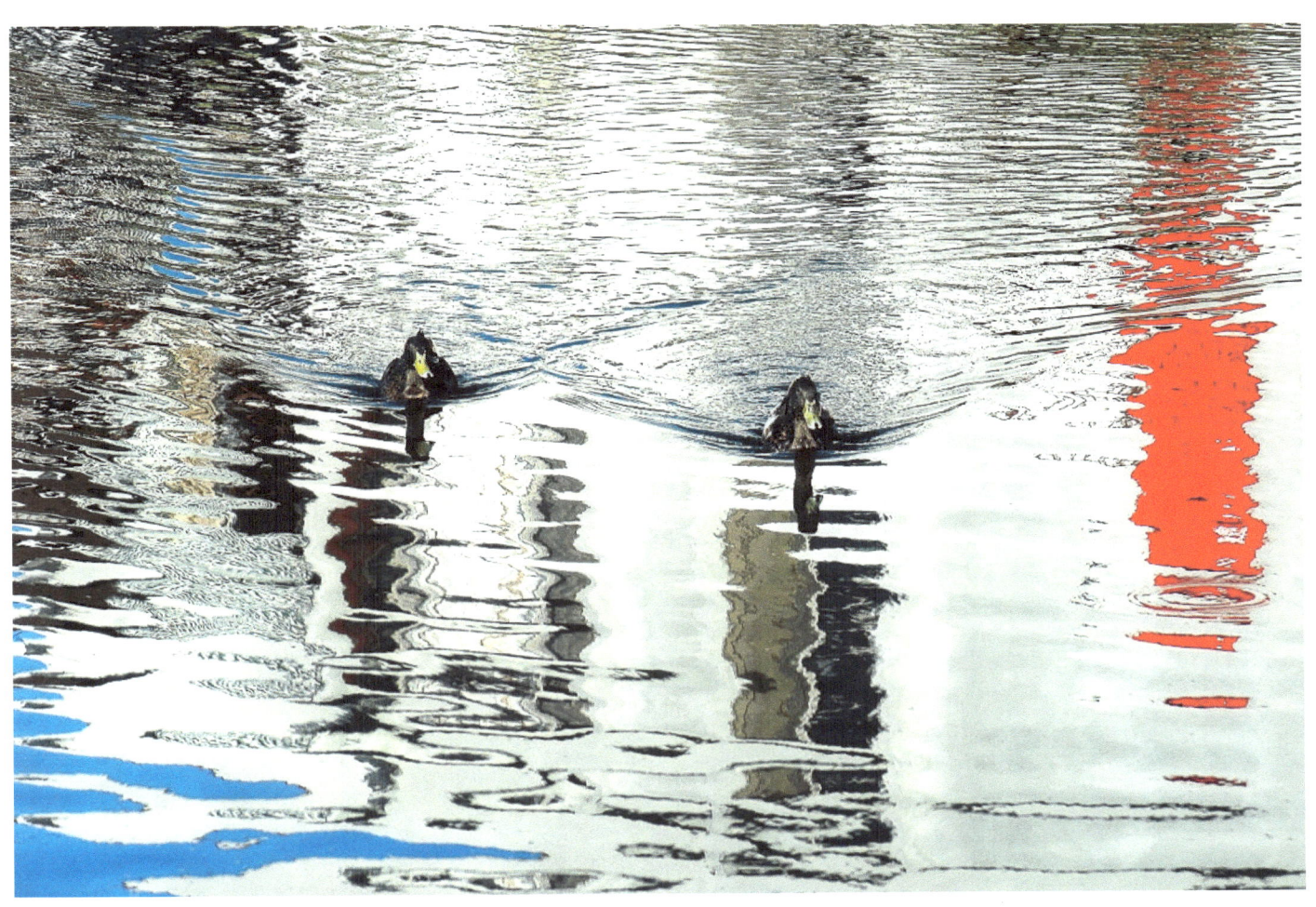

Abstract Life

Quietly moving, constantly morphing; never the same from one ripple to the next.

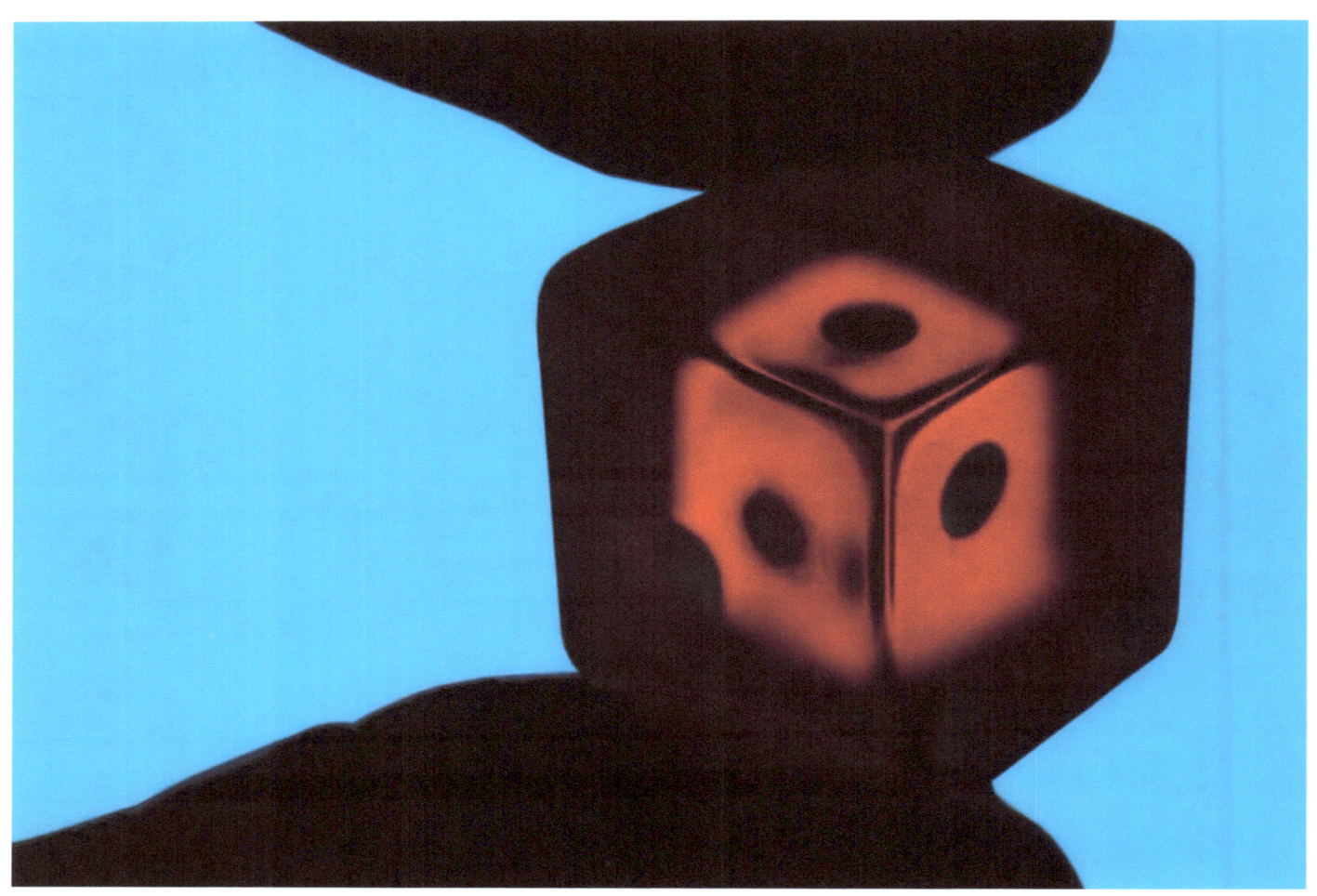

Thirds

The sum is always greater than the parts.

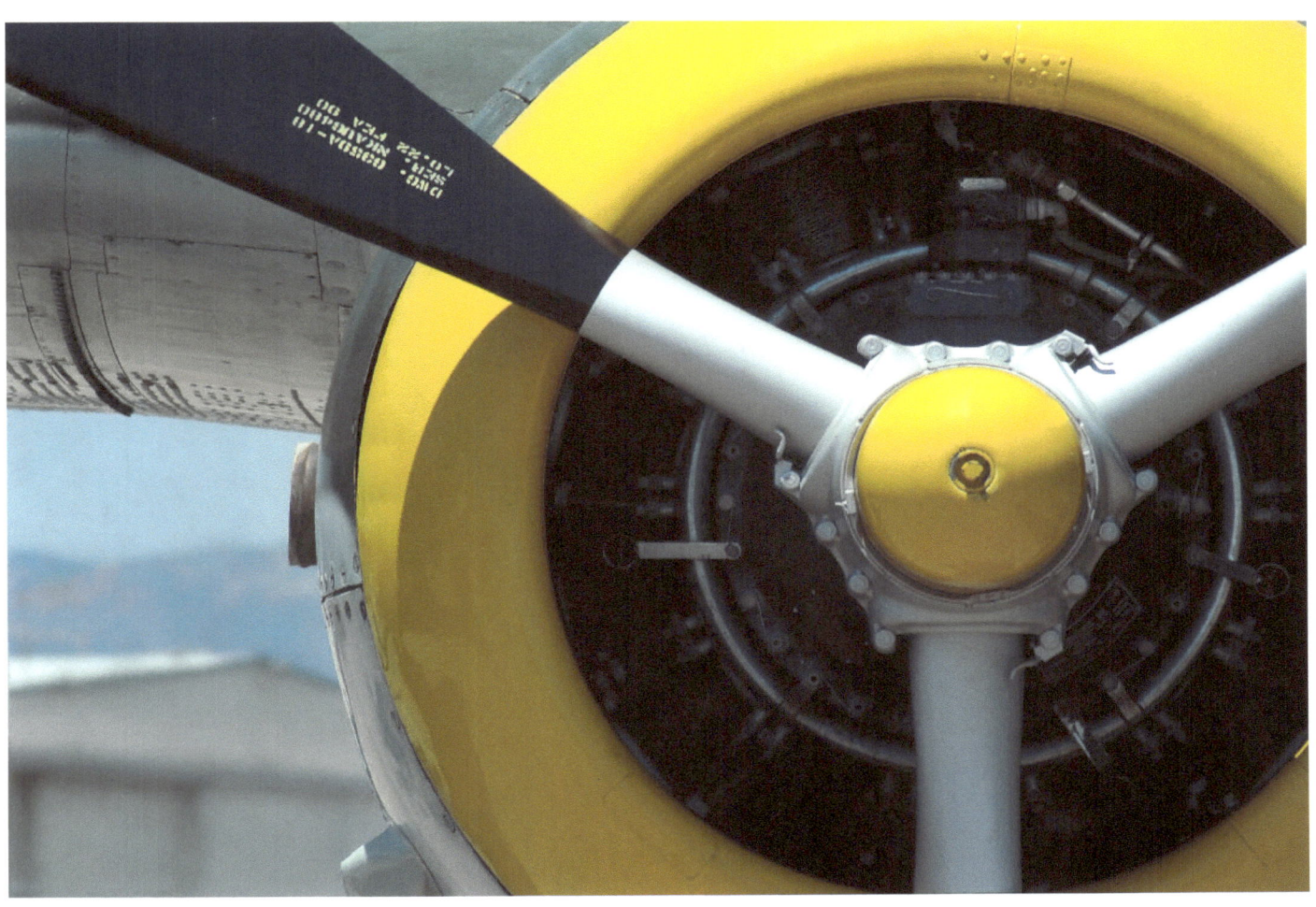

Prop

Color, mechanics and design; three things that help this simple idea fly.

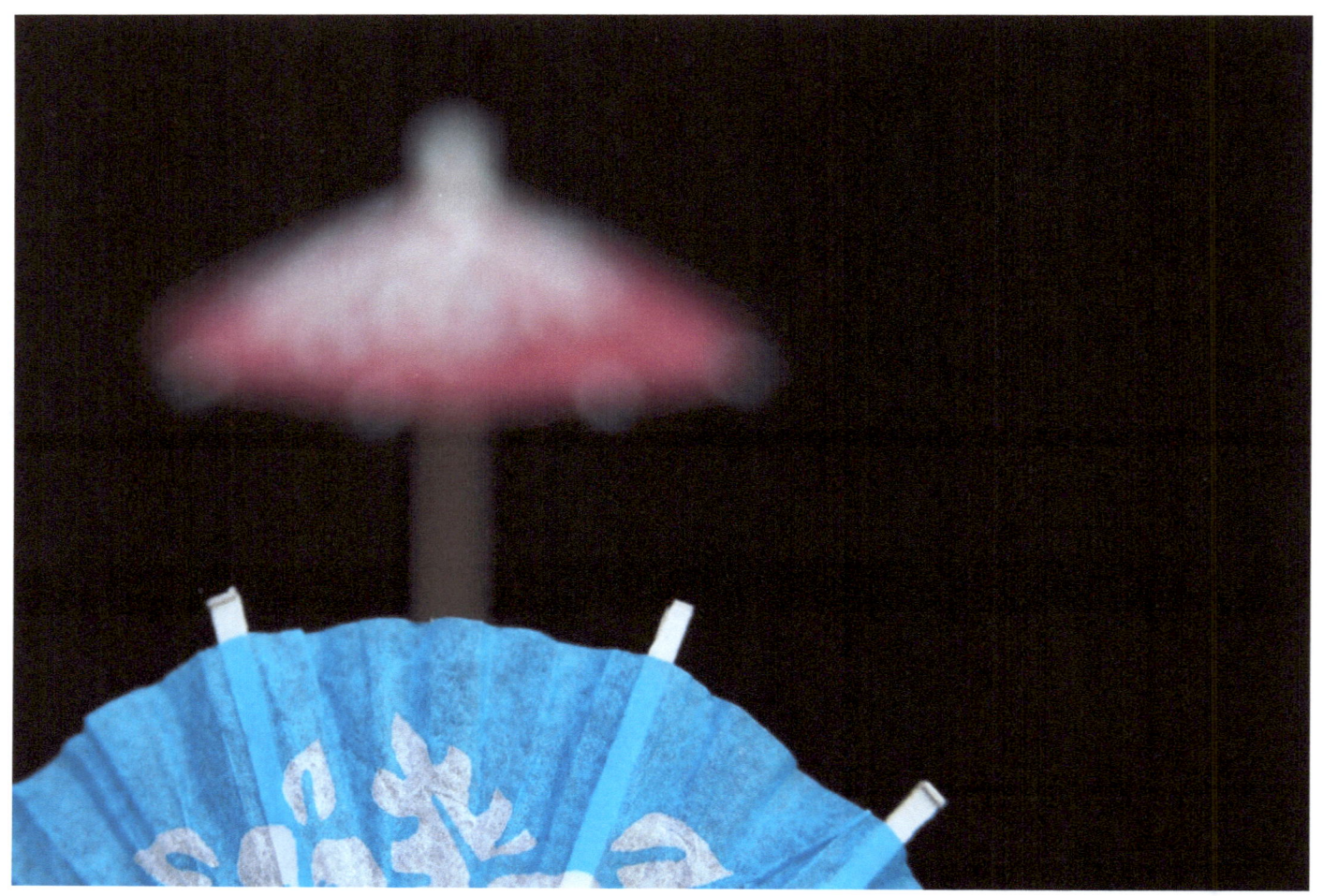

Paper Thin

Fragile elements, strong impression.

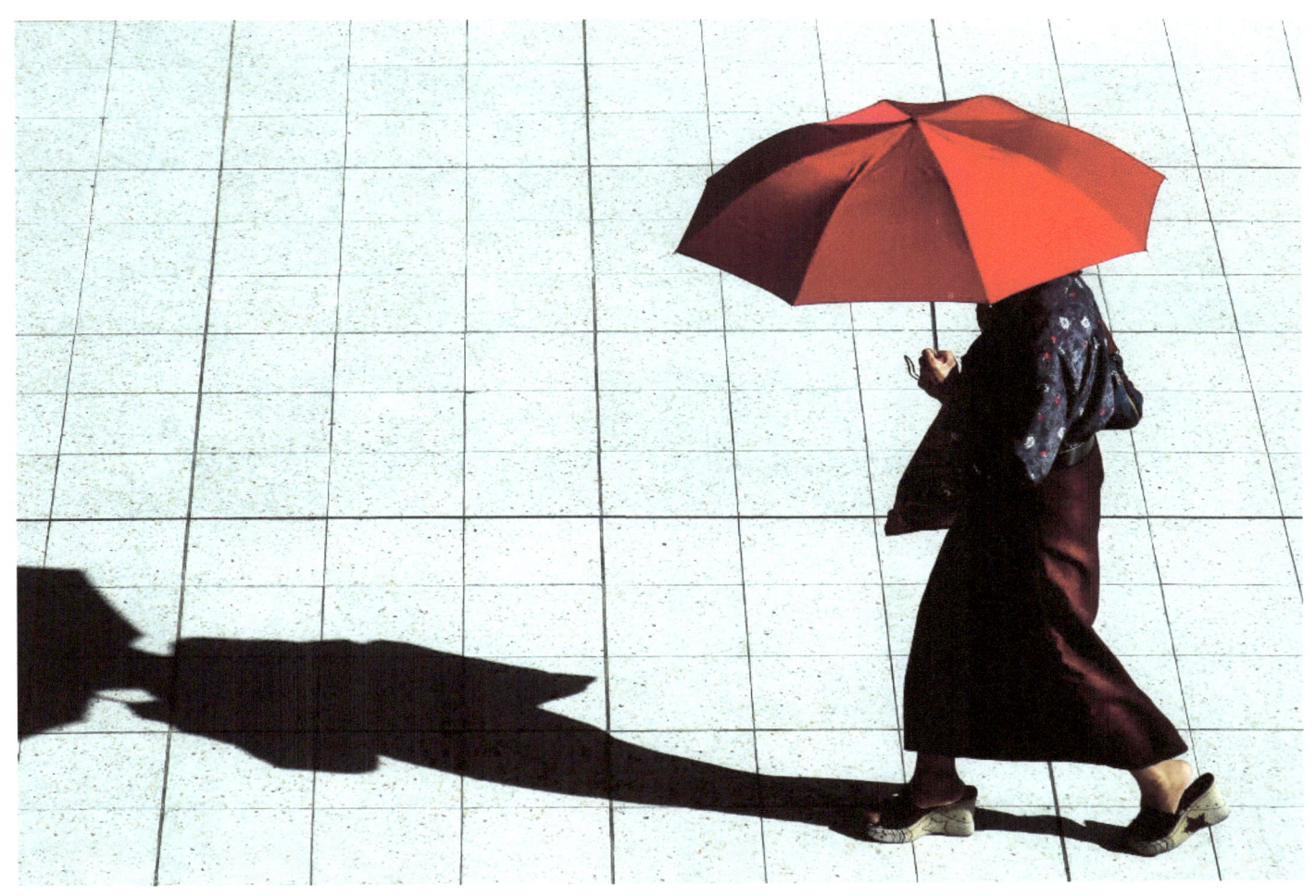

Sunny Day

A red parasol brightens a sunny day.

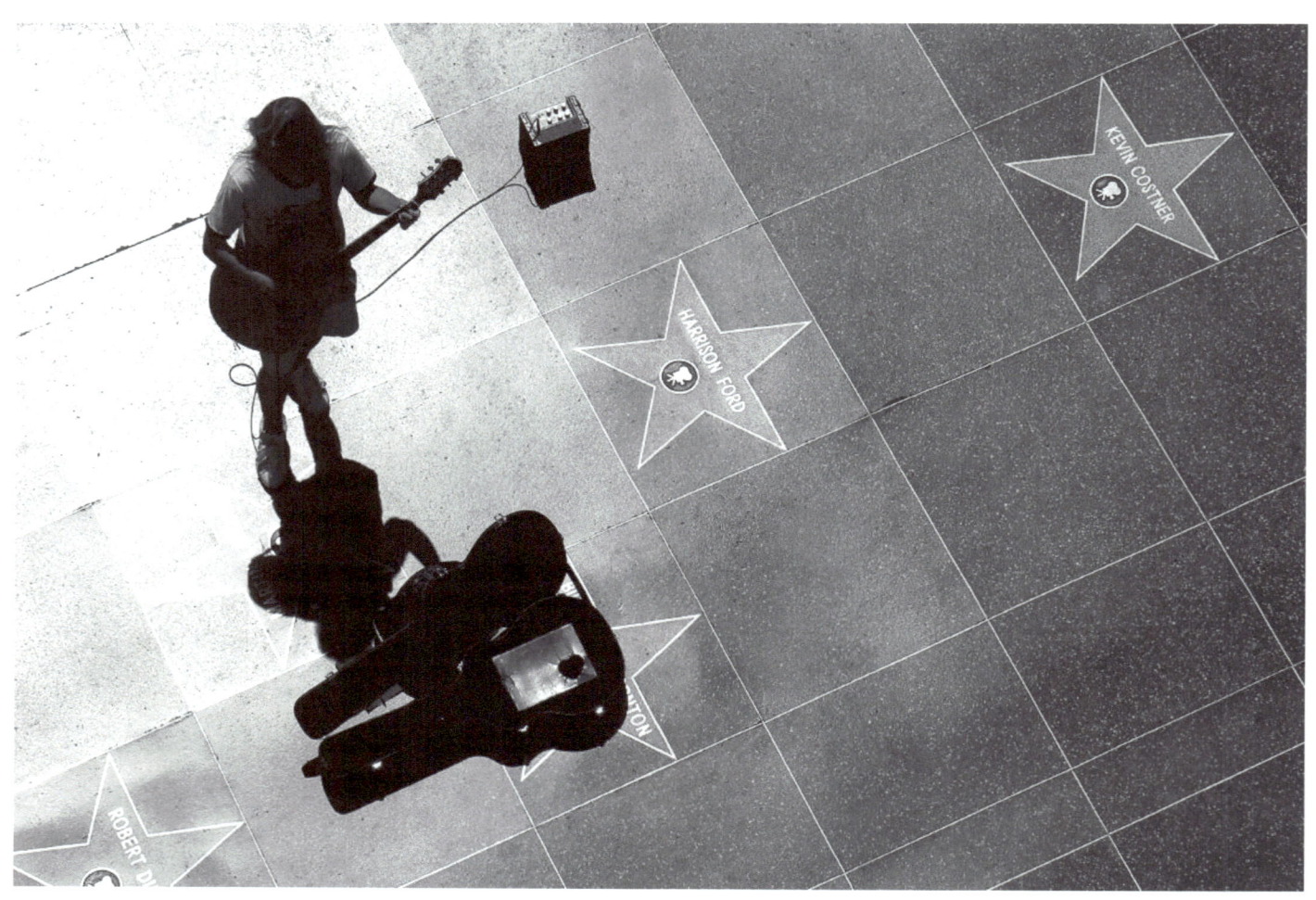

Starlight

If only for an afternoon, he found his place among the stars.

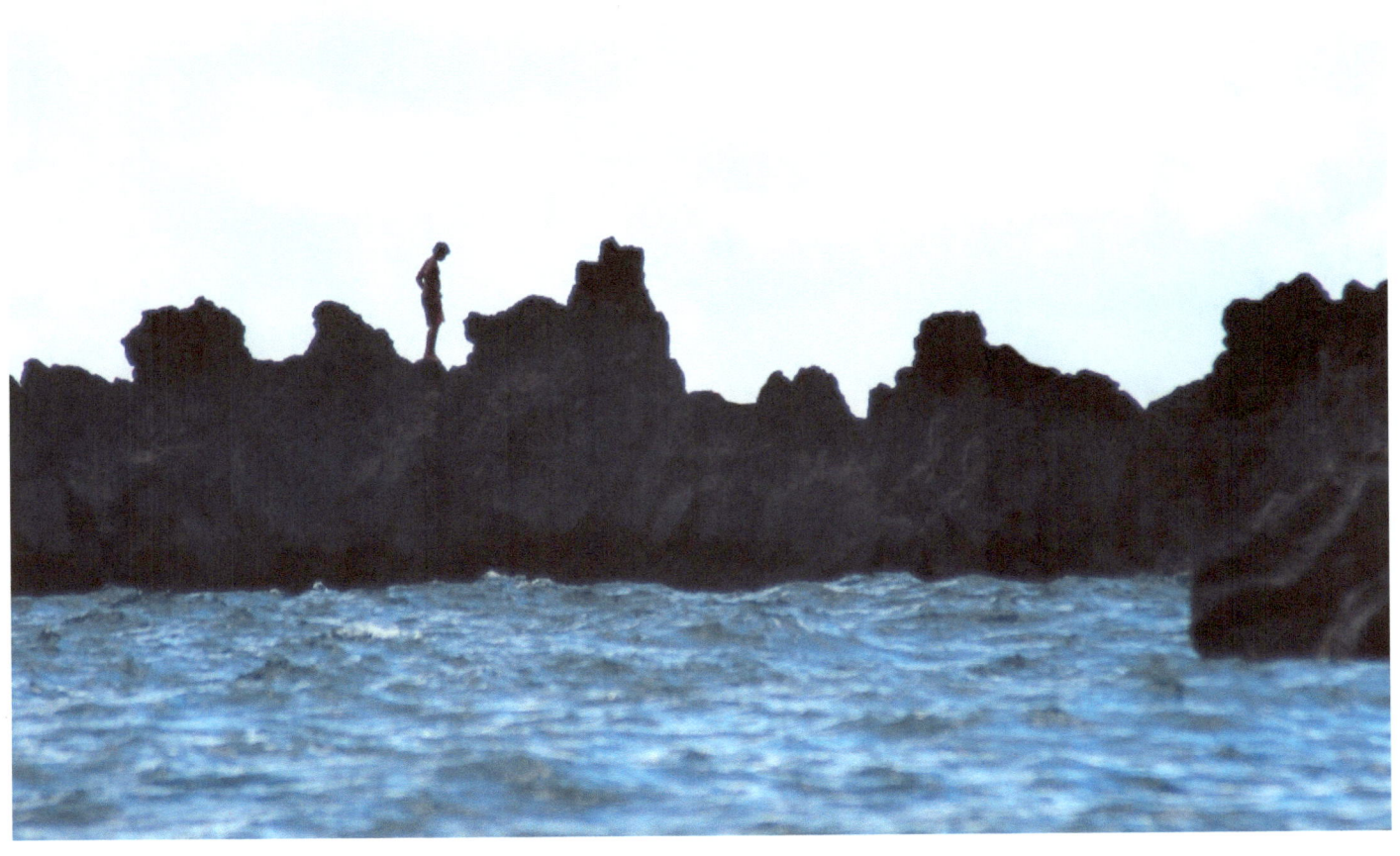

On The Rocks

Sometimes, blending in means becoming part of something bigger.

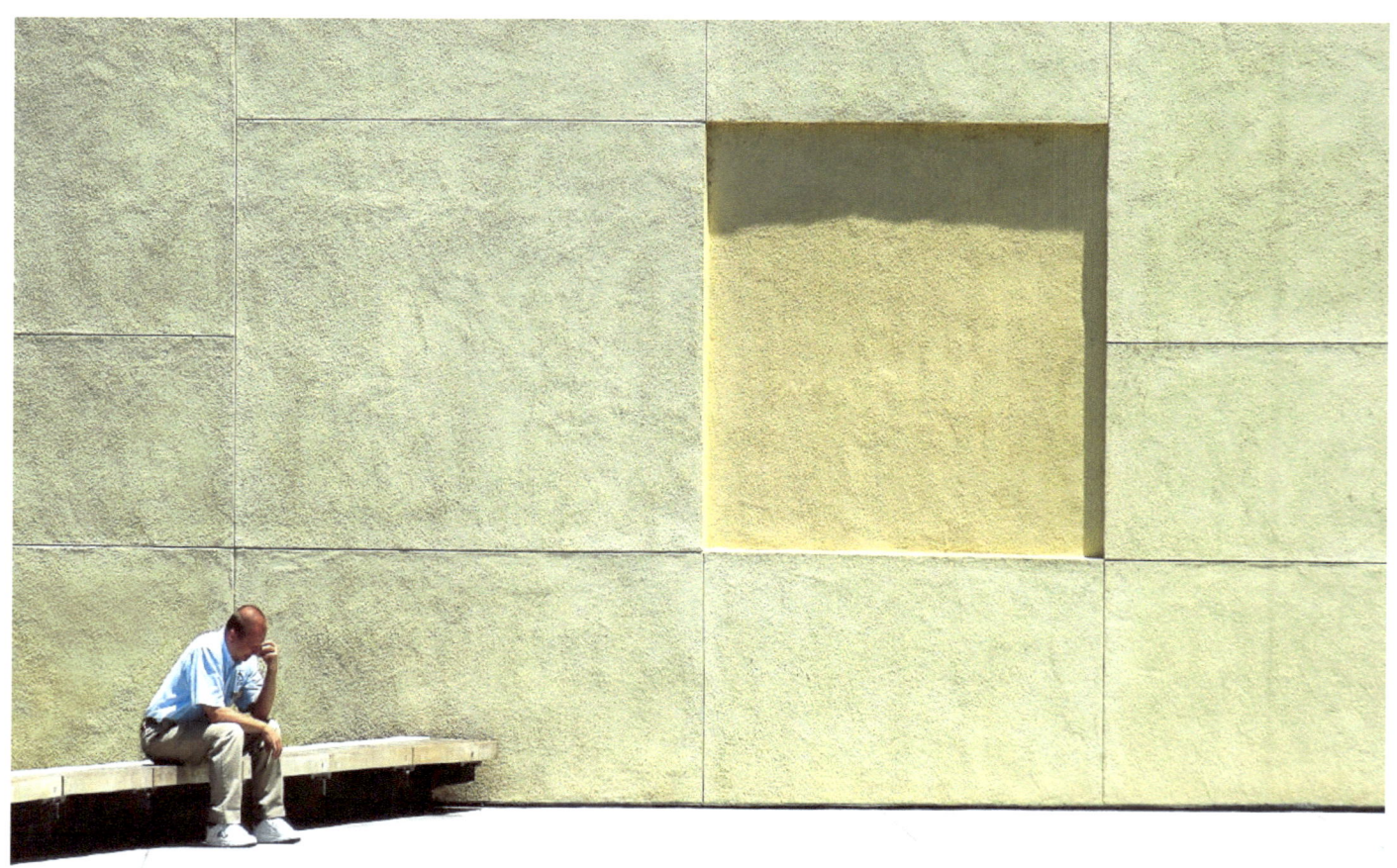

Outside The Box

Once he placed himself outside the box, he realized he was on his own.

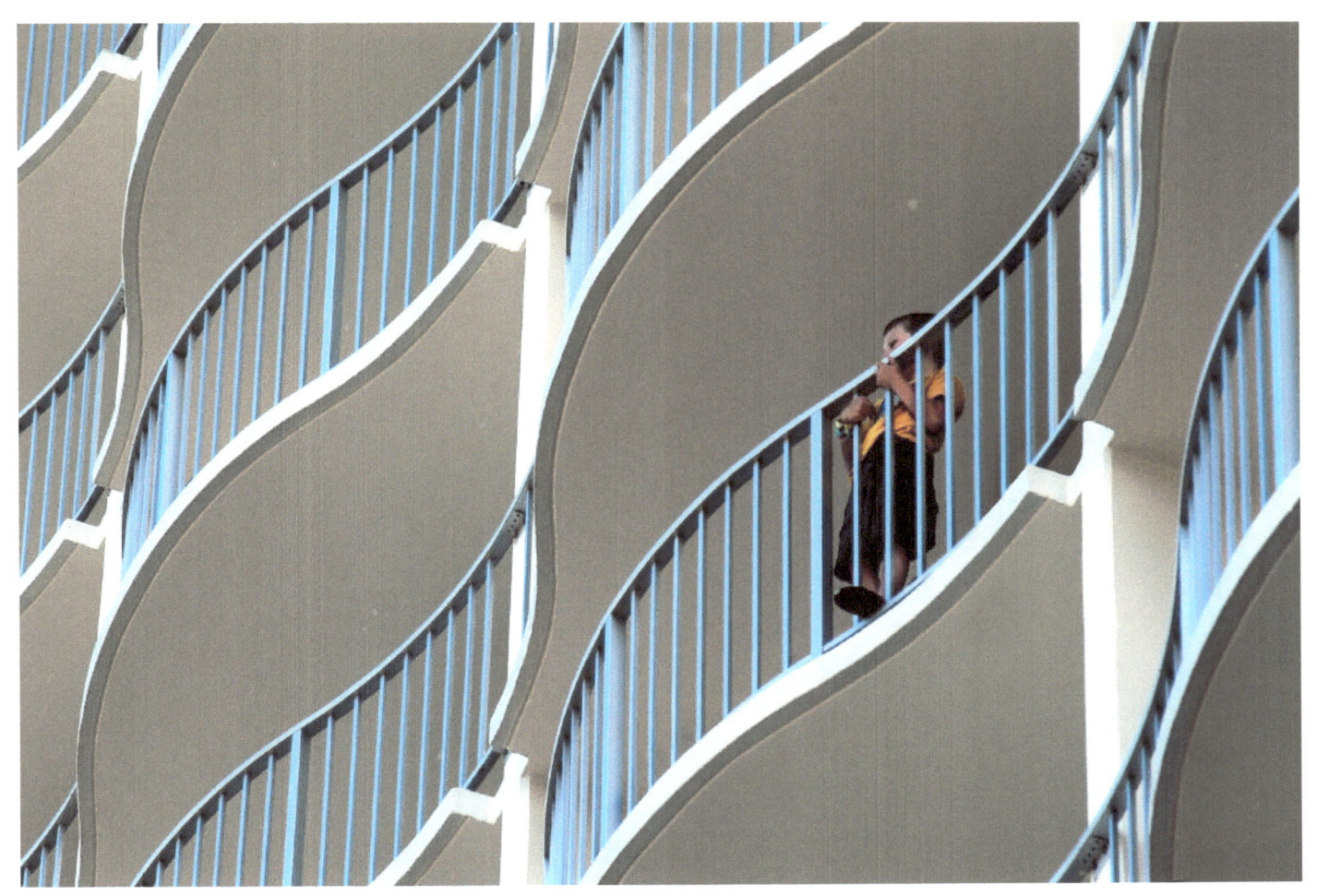

Prisoner By Design

To me, he was trapped between wrought iron and cement. For him, it was an opportunity to see farther than ever before.

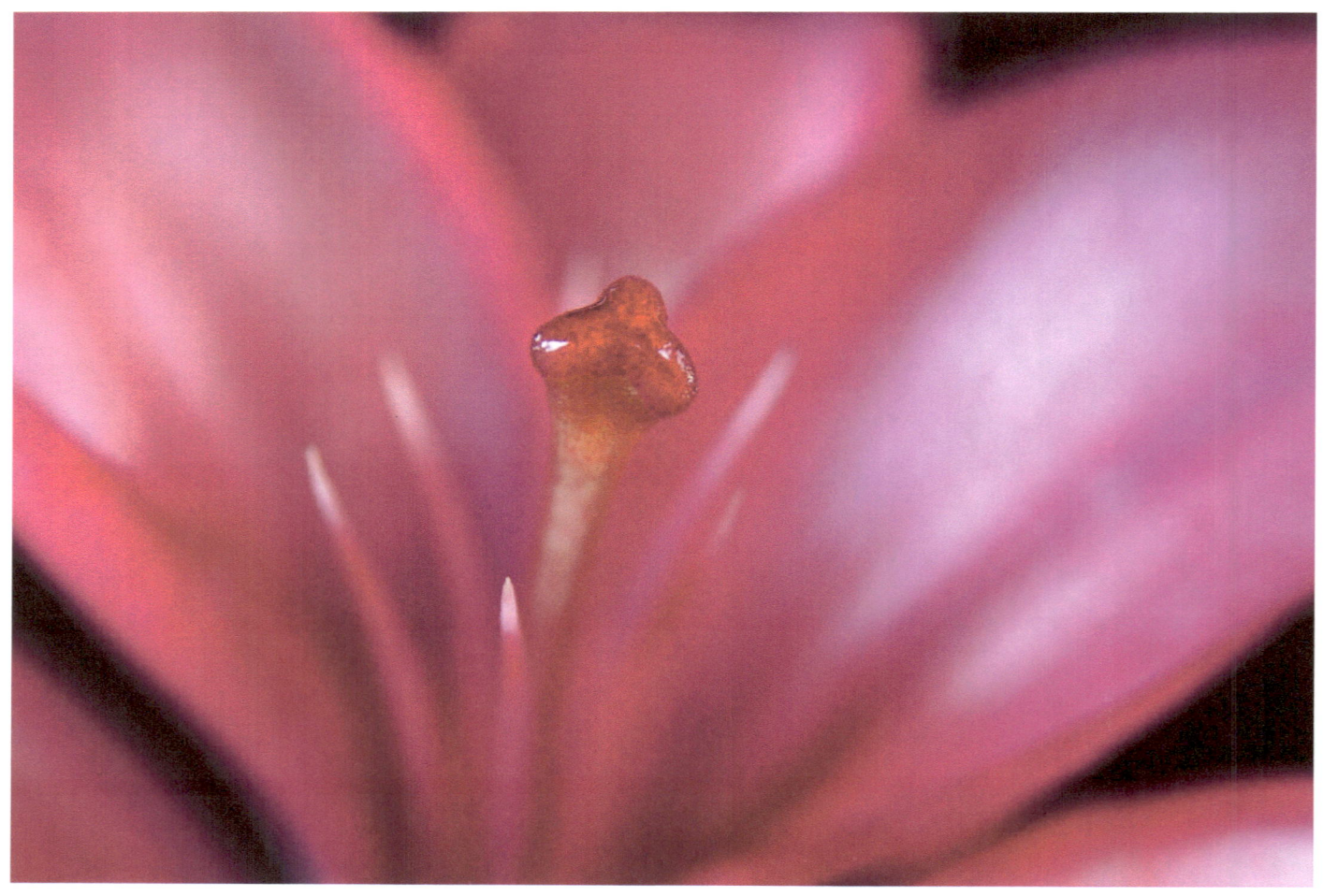

Passion

In the heart of the flower, passion blooms.

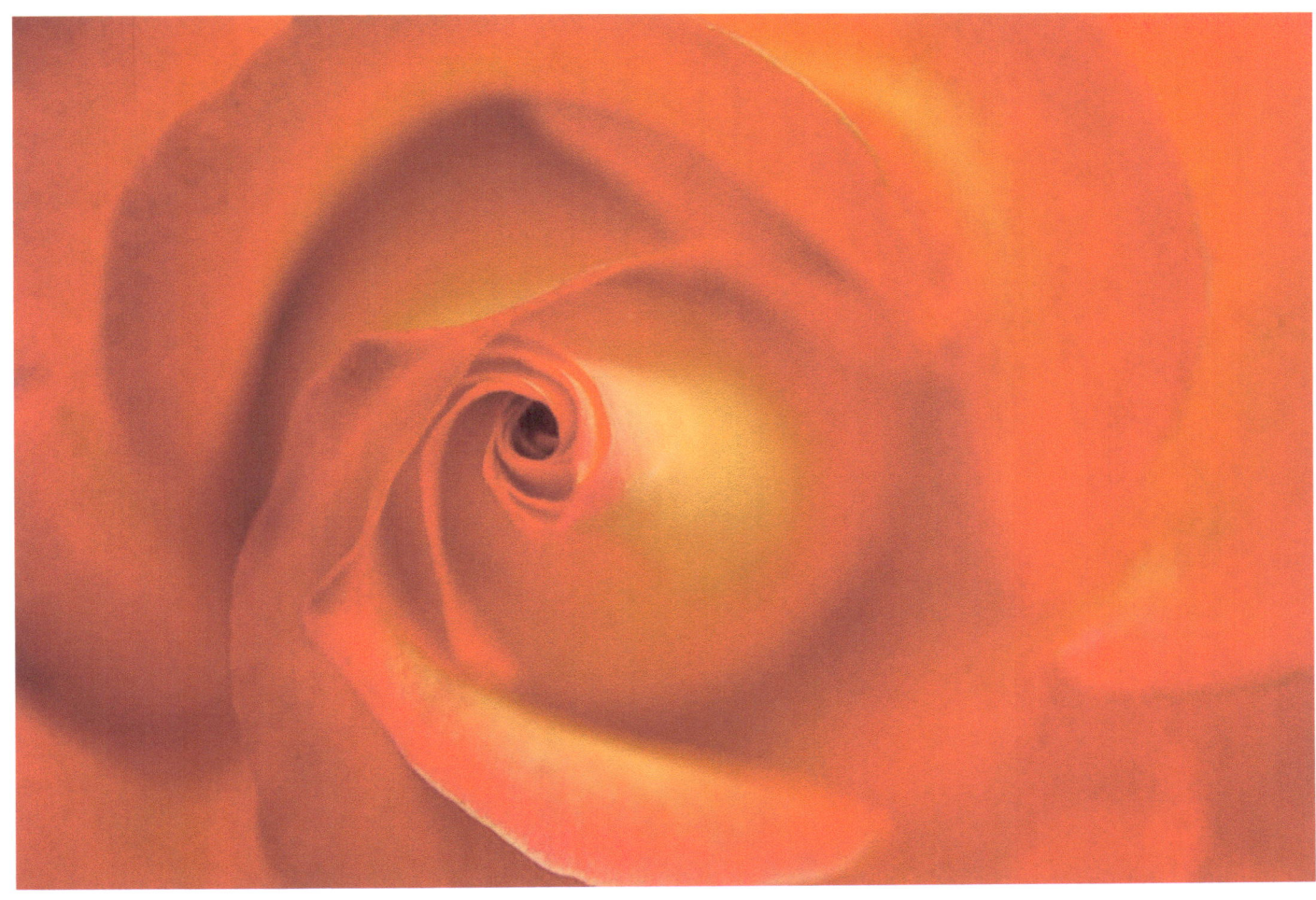

Vortex

Deep inside, I rediscovered something I had lost long ago.

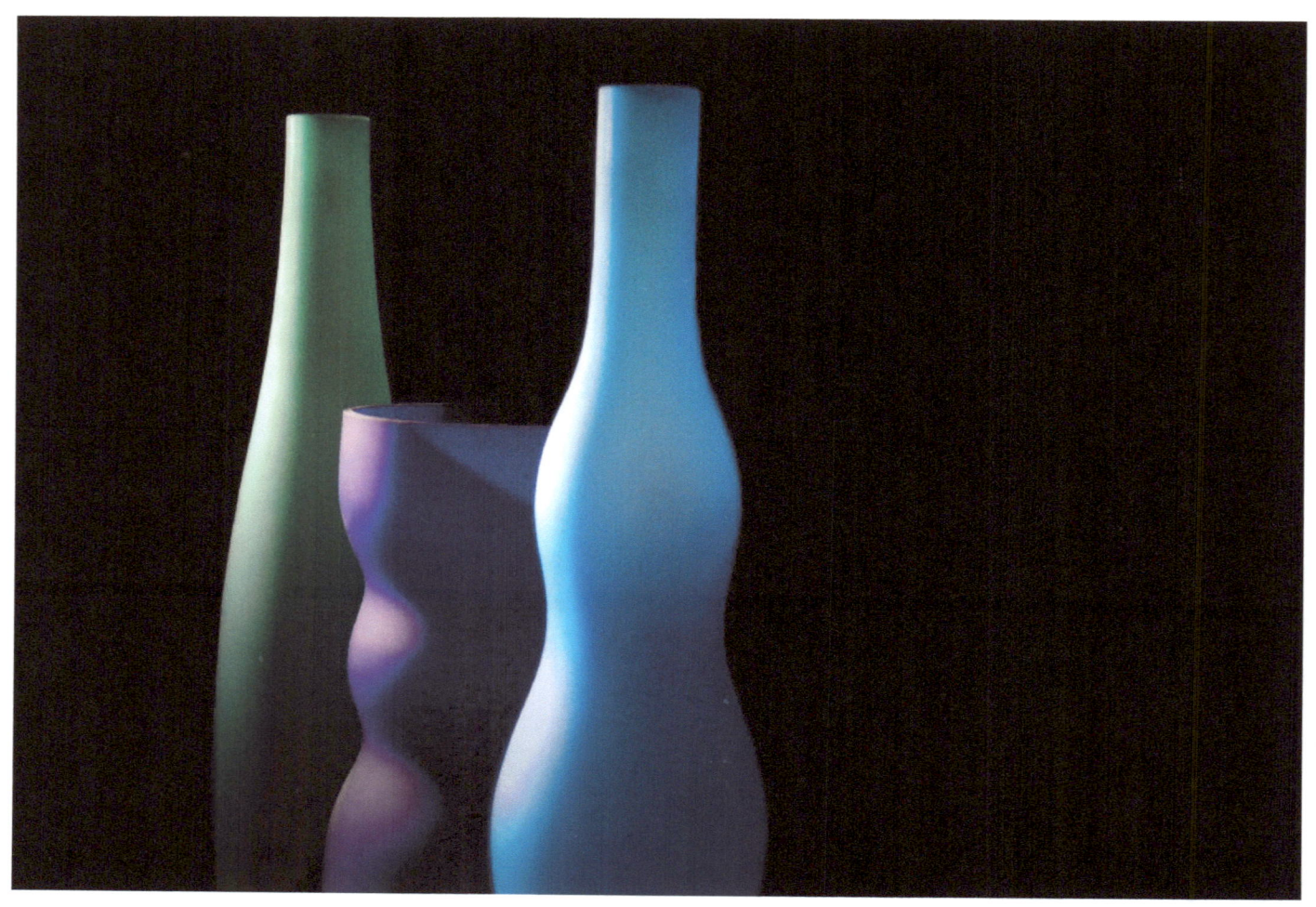

No Flowers

Three vases, no flowers.

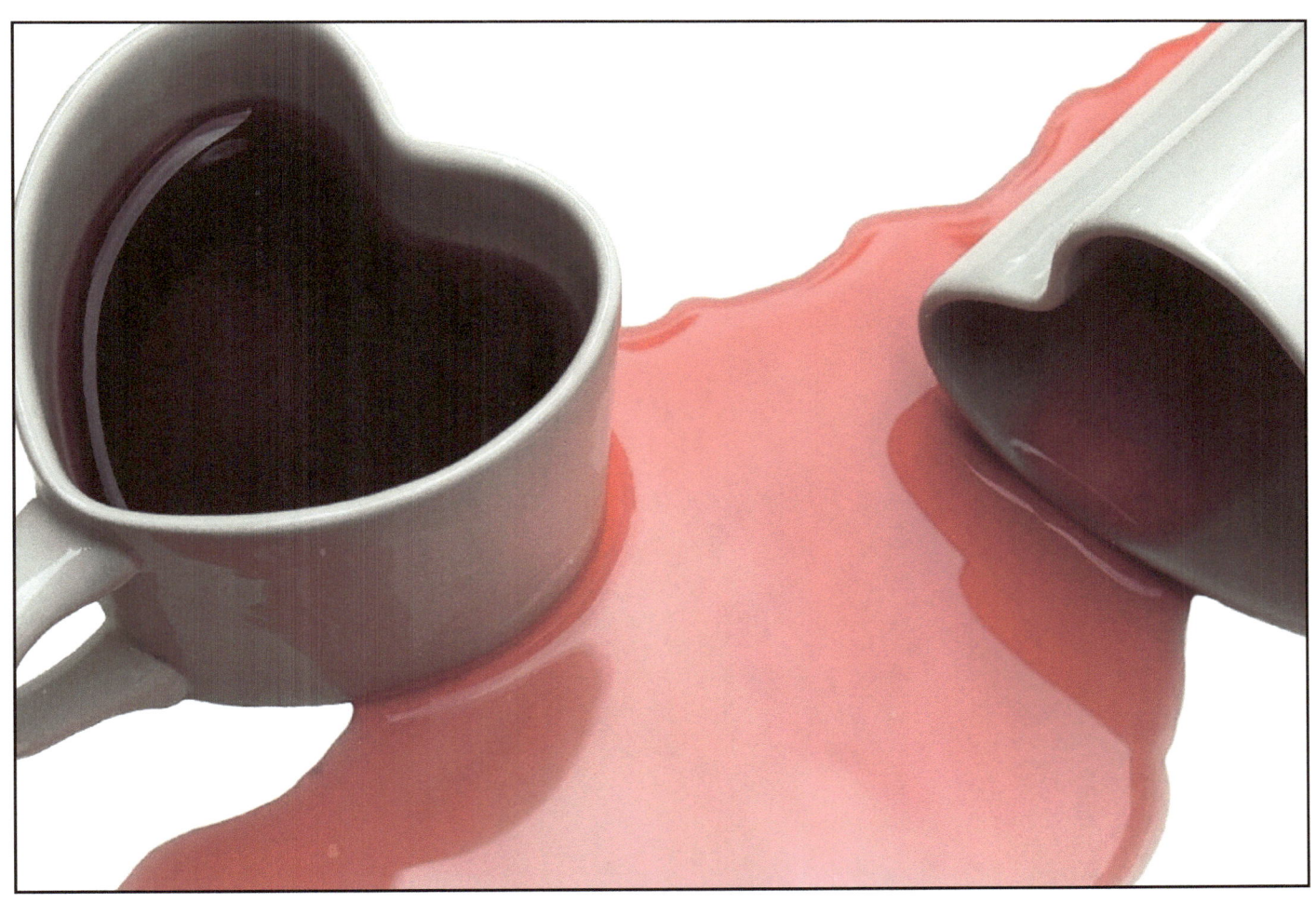

Love Story

An ancient story told every day for the very first time.

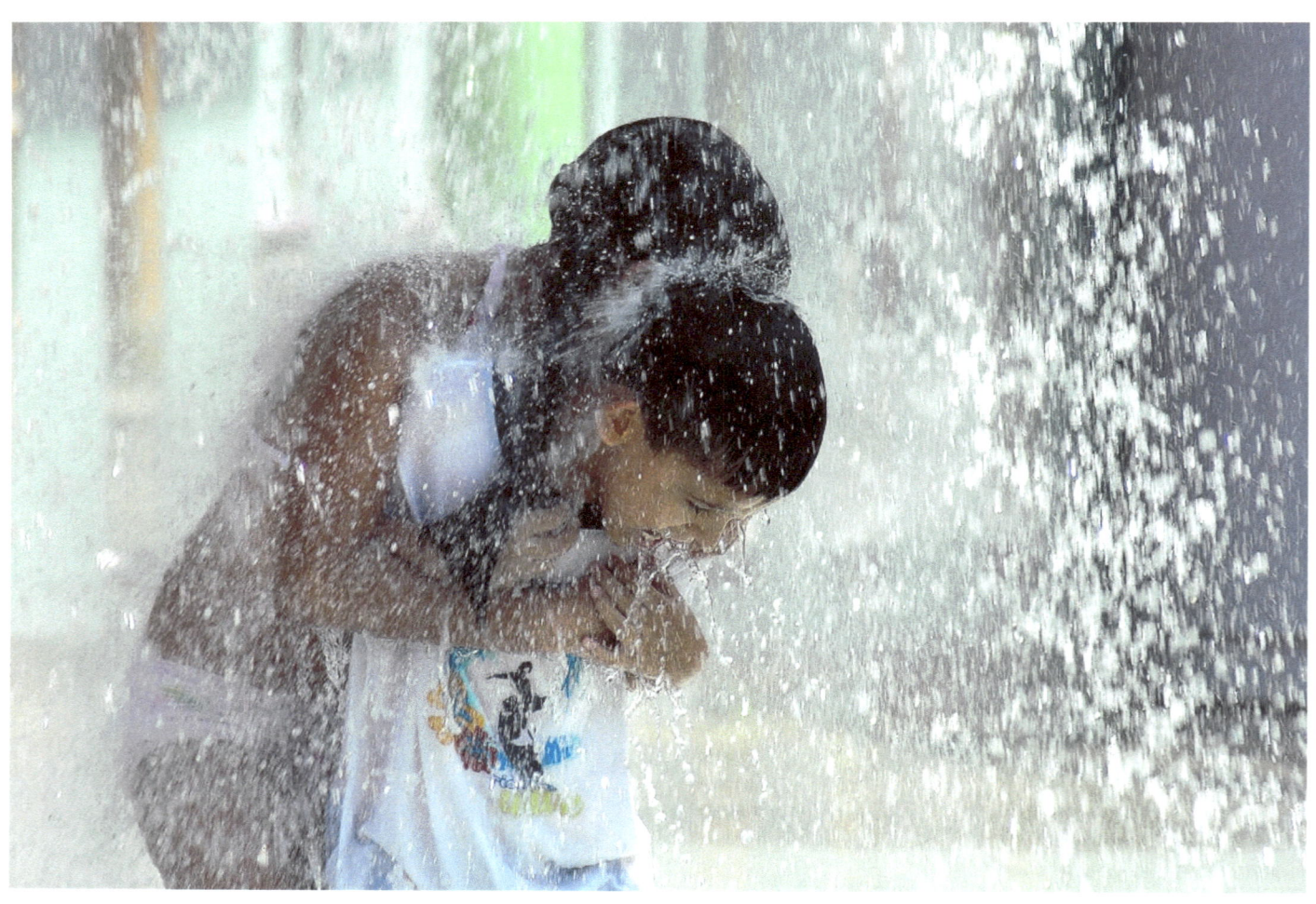

Hold On

He played along because it wasn't about staying dry, it was about letting his big sister get drenched.

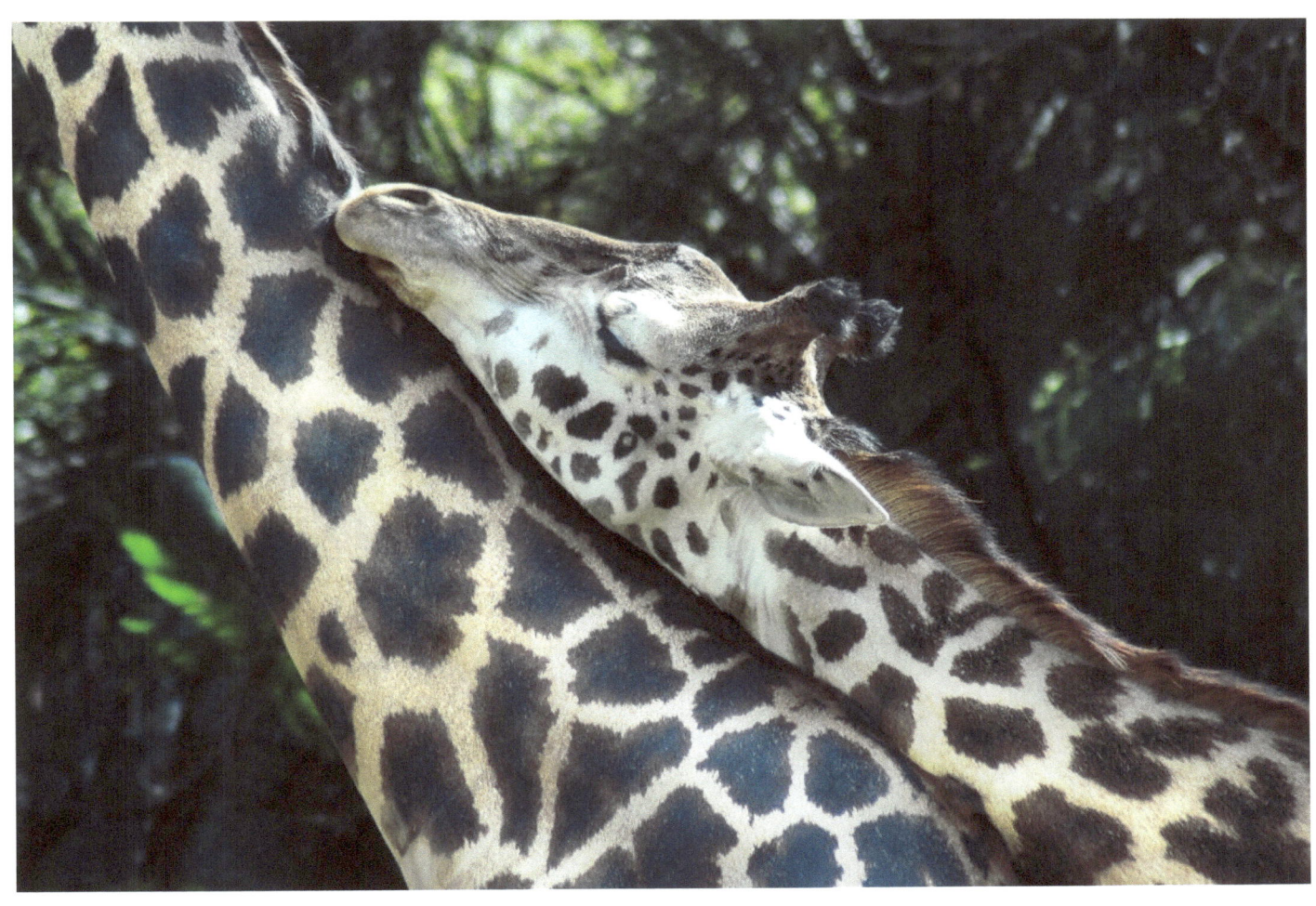

Love And Affection

Quality time with Mom.

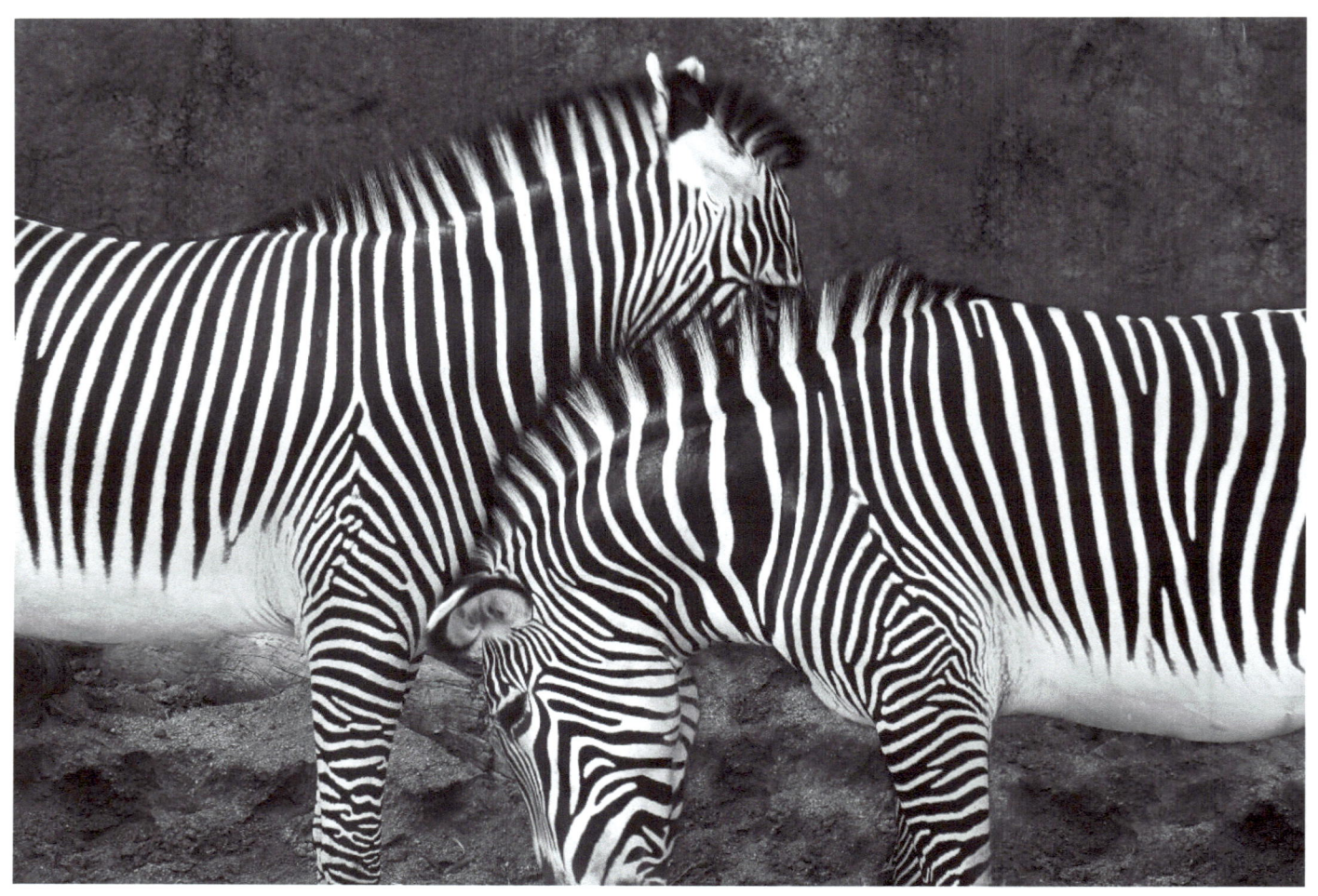

Different Stripes

Although they had different stripes, they had one thing in common: each other.

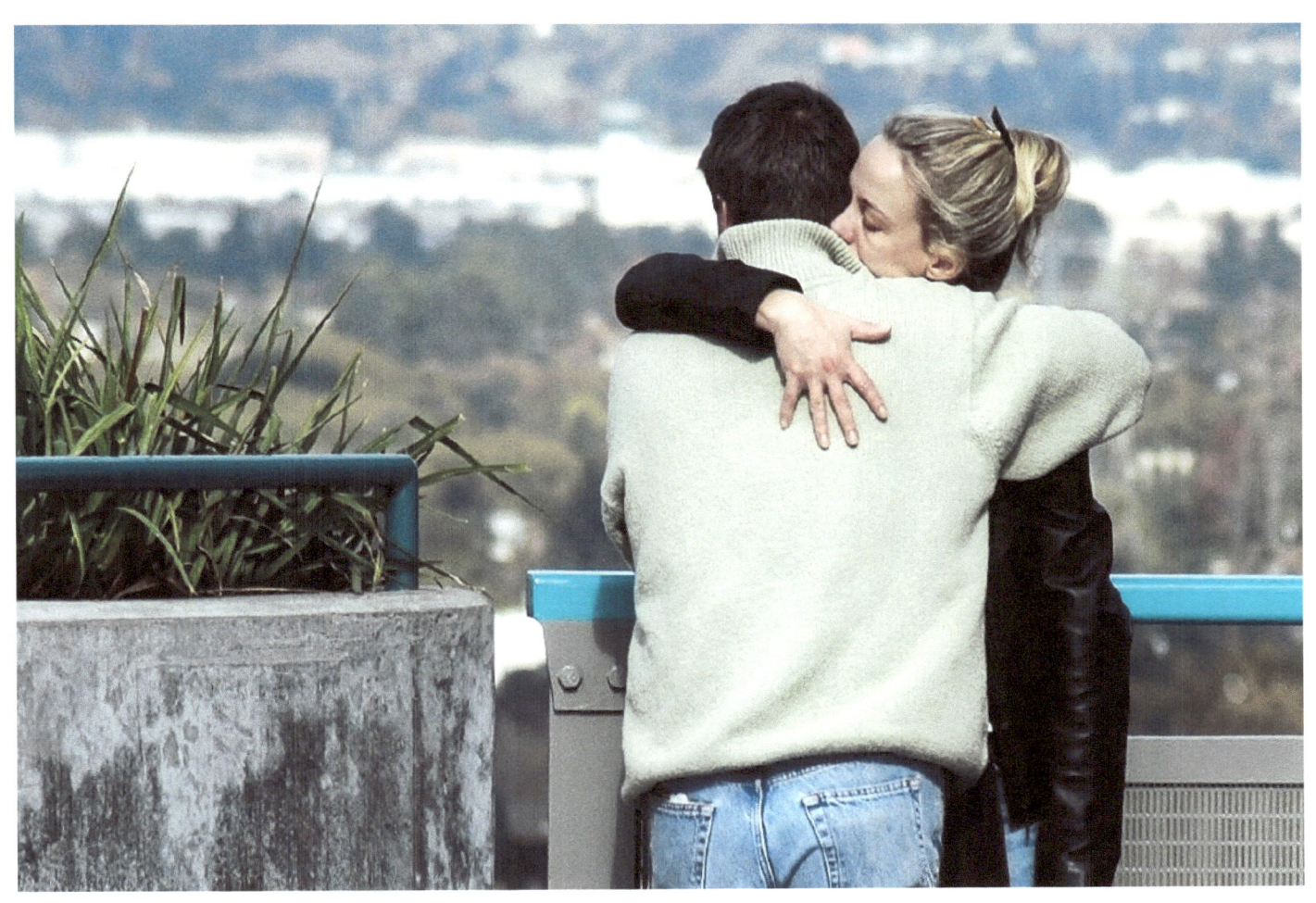

Without A Word

Most pictures speak for themselves but once in a while a picture shouts.

Dan Holm lives in Southern California and explores life through images and the stories they tell. He can be contacted at: dan@theholmpage.com